Dr Abby J Waterman is an 88-year-old retired consultant pathologist who has been a Harley Street dentist, an entrepreneur and director of a Cancer Research laboratory, as well as the mother of four children. She lives in London with her husband, while her children and grandchildren are scattered around the globe.

Also by Dr Abby J Waterman

Woman in a White Coat

(A Memoir)

Abby's Tales of Then and Now

by

Dr Abby J Waterman

Cover design by Nathan Burton

ISBN 9798649294300

A Doberman Elliott Associates Book

As ever for the real Joshua, the children, their partners
and the grandchildren
I love you all

Feel free to post comments on my blog https://abbyjw.com or email me at abbyjwaterman@btinternet.com.

CONTENTS

FOREWORD

I thought that as an 88 year old, social media was not for me. However, especially now, during the coronavirus pandemic, it has been a lifeline while my husband, Josh, has been the only person I have spoken to up-close for the best part of four months.

Intending to use this quiet time to write a sequel to my memoir, I have instead become captivated by the pleasure of posting and interacting with so many people, making new friends with readers all over the world. Our younger son called to say he enjoyed my memoir, *Woman in a White Coat*, even more second time around, and encouraged me to post the pieces I was writing on *London, East End, Jewish*, my old school, *Central Foundation School for Girls* and various *Author* groups.

I wrote the first of these in August 2019 and the last in August 2020, so the later posts were written while self-isolating with Josh. We are both elderly and, with my medical history of a near-fatal heart attack and various auto-immune diseases, we are vulnerable and therefore shielding. We have only left home to drive to Tate Britain or the Imperial War Museum for short walks on Sundays when London is particularly quiet, to take the car for its MOT test and recycle some electrical items at the dump.

The biggest difference - and pleasure - for me, between writing a memoir and posting on social media, has been the spontaneous and immediate response from my readers. Corrections by those better informed than me have been very welcome.

1. NACHES AND YICHUS

So much naches and yichus (the joy from family, especially children). Our younger son rang to say he was re-reading my memoir 'Woman in a White Coat' and enjoying it even more second time around. Mine is the story of a poor orthodox Jewish girl growing up in London's East End, finally becoming a consultant pathologist in a major London teaching hospital, as well as a wife and mother of four children.

It made him laugh - and cry!

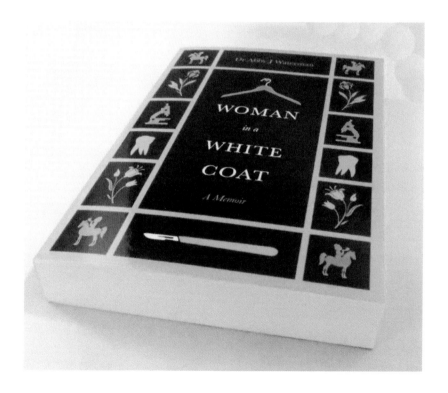

2. MEMORIES OF PETTICOAT LANE

Now blocked by a shutter and covered with graffiti, we entered via the Goulston Street entrance to 116 Wentworth Dwellings, where we lived until 1942.

We children never knew the dark history of the landing above ours. It wasn't until I started to research the history of Petticoat Lane for my memoir *'Woman in a White Coat'*, that I discovered that in the doorway of 119 Wentworth Dwellings, two floors above us, at 2.55 am on Sunday September 30th, 1888, PC Long found a blood-soaked piece of Catherine Eddowes' apron. Her murderer, thought to be *Jack the Ripper,* had left her mutilated body in Mitre Street, some distance away. His reign of terror in the East End of London, killing and disembowelling local prostitutes, finally ended with the murder of Mary Jane Kelly.

Had we known it then, I'm sure we'd have played *Jack the Ripper* games instead of *'Cops and Robbers'* or *'Doctors and Nurses'*.

Our flat was on the third floor on the right

3. ON HAVING A CAT

I'd love to have a cat now we're getting on for 90 and don't go abroad anymore. We don't enjoy long airplane flights and schlepping our all-too-heavy baggage around, but we live on the 9th floor with a balcony and I couldn't face a repeat of my experience with Rupert when I was a child, and lived on the third floor with a balcony in Wentworth Dwellings in Petticoat Lane.

Rupert was a gorgeous black kitten who was as curious as all baby animals are. It was wonderful coming home from school to be greeted by Rupert. He would wind himself round and round my ankles, delighted to see me again.

When I went to the toilet on our little balcony, Rupert would follow me and walk along the brick support at the bottom of the protective railings. As he grew bolder, he started climbing over the coal bunker and up to the bar at the top, weaving in and out of the upright spikes. I could hardly bear to watch him. Sometimes he walked along the railings to our neighbour's balcony. She usually had a few scraps for a cat who was always hungry, even when he had just been fed.

'Be careful,' I told Rupert. 'I know you've got nine lives, but we're on the third floor, and it's a long way down.'

Rupert said nothing and stalked into the kitchen, but when I did my homework he came to sit on my lap, purring loudly.

One day, when I was standing on the balcony watching as Rupert put one careful foot in front of the other on the top bar of the guard rail, my mother called me.

'Abby, come in at once. What's all this?' she said, pointing to the scrunched-up drawings I'd left on the kitchen table.

As I turned towards her, Rupert lost his footing and fell. I was paralysed; couldn't move.

'Mummy, come quickly,' I screamed. 'Rupert's fallen off.'

'He'll be dead, for sure, but you'd better go down and see.'

I raced down the six flights of stairs, out into Goulston Street, round into Wentworth Street and into the entrance of our courtyard. Rupert was sitting there, nonchalantly licking a paw, as if falling from the third floor was nothing.

'You're a naughty, naughty, kitten,' I said, as I picked him up and hugged him.

The nosy old woman who was always sitting on her first-floor balcony, looking out and gossiping about everyone, said:

'They've got nine lives and no mistake. You should look after it better, Abby. You tell your mother I said so.'

Rupert licked my hand with his rough little tongue.

'You're to stop walking along the railings,' I told him.

But an hour later he was winding in and out of the spikes again, as if to show he wasn't a scaredy cat, even if I was.

4. MOTHER LEVY'S HOME

I was born in what was known as 'Mother Levy's Home', in 1931. It was not an auspicious time to be born - in the midst of the Great Depression, with my father out of work. The Jewish Maternity Hospital was at 24-26 Underwood Street, Whitechapel, 1911-1947. Not being a boy, I was a great disappointment – who wanted a third daughter? It may not have been within the sound of Bow Bells – so maybe I'm an EastEnder rather than a real Cockney.

The late Sir Arnold Wesker – who was briefly my boyfriend in the late 40's - told me that he was delivered there a year after I was by the famous neurologist and writer Dr Oliver Sachs but maybe it was another Dr Sachs, his sister.

Image of The Jewish Maternity Hospital from 'The Gentle Author' in the profile of Tom Ridge

5. HOW THE OTHER HALF LIVES

After I left Wentworth Dwellings in 1956 to get married, my parents moved to a smaller flat in Carter House, Brune Street. Carter House was named after Ernest Carter, the vicar who led the hymns on the Titanic as it was sinking (*The Gentle Author*).

There, for the first time, they had a bath – but not a bathroom. The bath was along one side of the tiny kitchen but since there was only a cold water tap with no Ascot or other hot water heater, it had to be filled with lots and lots of kettles or large saucepans of water heated on the gas stove. It was hopeless.

My parents covered the wooden lid with oilcloth, where it formed their only work surface and they carried on going to Goulston Street baths.

Later, when I was a medical student and studying with a group of young people who had all been to public school, I overheard one say 'It's a waste of time providing the poor with baths. They only use them to keep coal!!'

My parents never did that, but what else was the bath good for? I wonder how many people were scalded carrying boiling water back and forth!!

Carter House where my parents moved after I got married

6. MINIATURE BLOOD-PUMP TO CURE HEART FAILURE

If it makes its way through all the clinical trials and into production, the amazing Israeli instrument from Magenta Medical 'Left Ventricular Assist Device' could save lives, allowing heart muscles to rest while still pumping blood. The idea is that the pump is then removed once the heart is repaired. As the rate of heart disease in developed countries continues to skyrocket, the progress of this little device is definitely something to watch.

I could have done with the Israeli invention 4 years ago, when I had a major heart attack. I was on a ventilator and needed to have a pump inserted into my aorta – the largest artery in the body – to help my failing heart. The actual pump mechanism was at the foot of my bed and quite noisy. Like 80% of patients in ICU, when I wasn't comatose I was delirious. The air conditioning vent in the ceiling above my head was circular and the noise of the pump convinced me that it was the port of a washing machine. I expected to be drenched any minute.

After I left hospital the consultant emailed me to say I could get help if the memories of my delusions and hallucinations was upsetting.

'Not at all', I replied. 'It will make a perfect last chapter for my memoir *Woman in a White Coat.*

The ceiling vent I was sure was the door to a washing machine

7. SPITALFIELDS FRUIT AND VEGETABLE MARKET AND CFS

'Can you put it under your chin?', 'Give us a kiss and I'll carry that great thing for you,' were the more polite things that were shouted at me by the market porters – huge towers of circular baskets balanced on their heads – as I wended my way carrying my cello, between squashed vegetables and piles of horse droppings on my way to Central Foundation Girls School (CFS) in Spital Square, on the edge of Spitalfields market,. A school leaver, now a professional musician, had donated her old practice cello to the school and I'd been chosen to learn to play.

It was quite sad, going back so many years later, and seeing it all gone, replaced by a posh entrance and a mixture of some good and some tacky stalls and emporia. I had loved walking through that market – cheeky porters and underfoot debris and all.

Another historic site gentrified.

8 'EASY TIGER' at the Royal Academy London
Loved 'Easy Tiger' by Scottish brothers David and Robert Mach on display
at the Royal Academy 2019 Summer Show. The magnificent beast is covered
with wrappers from Tunnock's Tea Cakes, Viscount biscuits and Marks and
Spencer tea cakes.

A couple of weeks later this irresistible box of Tunnock's Tea Cakes caught my eye in the local Little Waitrose and I had to buy one – even though I'm on and off slimming.

9. THE FATE OF CENTRAL FOUNDATION SCHOOL FOR GIRLS

It was sad, going back in 2011 and seeing my old school, Central Foundation School for Girls, demolished, only the hall left standing with tacky temporary doors. I could picture the magnificent organ that I always wanted to learn, but was too shy to ask for lessons, and the bars up the walls at the sides for when the hall became the gym. There had been a platform at the end with the organ on one side, a lectern in the centre and on the other side a piano, on which I often played a voluntary before assembly on Mondays.

Then, when we returned in 2017, we found that the hall had been converted into a posh restaurant 'La Chapelle'. The maître d' kindly allowed us to look around. The essential structure remained with its lovely arched windows but it was a shame to see another London historical building gone.

Fortunately, Central Foundation School for Girls hasn't closed down but has transferred to Bow and is still going strong.

The Old CFS School Hall in 2013 before conversion to *La Chapelle* restaurant

10. WOMAN IN A WHITE COAT

My memoir *Woman in a White Coat* tells the story of the unwelcome third daughter of orthodox Jewish parents who desperately need a son to say the *kadesh* (prayer for the dead) at their funerals. She overcomes poverty and discrimination to become a Harley Street dentist, the co-founder of Conran-designed educational toyshops and, finally, a consultant pathologist and director of a Cancer Research laboratory.

Abby draws us a picture of what it was like growing up in a cold-water tenement in Petticoat Lane. She is torn from her family in WW2 to be evacuated to Littleport and Ely and then to Dawlish in South Devon. She returns to London only to endure the Blitz and later Hitler's V1 and then V2 rockets raining down.

We hear stories of her life as a dental student, a medical student and as a doctor, and read of the tears she sheds in private at the tragedies she sees. She buys a 'fortune' for twopence in Club Row and, as it predicts, she marries a fellow dentist, her loving companion for the next 60-odd years and has four wonderful children.

Woman in a White Coat is the story of triumph over adversity, the tale of a poor East End girl who makes good.

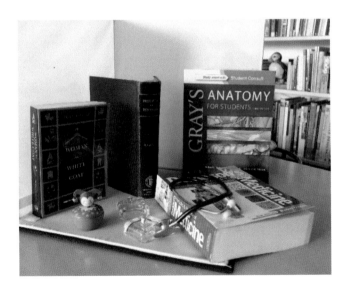

My memoir *Woman in a White Coat* and some 'light' medical reading

11. JEWS FREE INFANT SCHOOL

I started at Jews Free Infant School when I was three years old, going in via the entrance in Toynbee Street. My elder sister had already taught me to read and except for the afternoon naps I loved school from the first.

We had to take down the smelly rubber-covered mattresses and lie down in the dark with the curtains drawn. It was a daily ordeal and I hated lying there, sure I'd never get to sleep, but of course I soon drifted off.

Tour guides often show an entrance in Commercial Street but I never went in that way. It was sad seeing the now tacky Toynbee Street entrance when I went back in 2011.

12. FRYING PAN ALLEY

I moved up to Jews Free Junior School from Jews Free Infant School when I was seven but I wasn't there very long before being evacuated to Littleport and then to Ely. We were evacuated on September 1st - two days before WW2 was declared on September 3rd 1939. Upwards of 1 million children were evacuated on that day.

The entrance to our school was in Frying Pan Alley, a turning off Bell Lane. On one side was the school and on the other there were salmon smokeries. The smell was delicious as you left school to go home for your dinner (not called lunch then), but cloying and heavy on the way back after you'd eaten and were full.

I have few memories of my time there. I remember break time and the crates of milk stacked in the playground to be drunk before we went back in. Some children hated milk and had to find someone to drink theirs for them. June and I became firm friends over the milk. Maybe some of the children were unknowingly lactose intolerant and had a good reason for not wanting to drink milk.

I didn't care at all for the new characterless buildings in Frying Pan Alley when I went back in 2011. We had quite good coffee in the cafe on the corner but I'd rather have had one of the smoked salmon tasters you might be given on your way home by one of the men working in the smokeries.

13. EVACUATION SEPTEMBER 1st 1939 WW2

Upwards of a million children were evacuated from places thought to be potential targets on Friday September 1st 1939 – two days before war was declared. My middle sister had just won a Supplementary Scholarship to Central Foundation School for Girls and I was at Jews Free Junior School. Both of us were evacuated to Ely. We were sent first to a farm outside Littleport, then to a cottage in the village and finally to a semi-detached house on the outskirts of Ely.

Parents of girls had been told to pack 1 spare vest, 1 pair of knickers, 1 petticoat, 1 slip, 1 blouse, 1 cardigan, a coat or Mackintosh, nightwear, a comb, towel, soap, face-cloth, boots or shoes and plimsolls – not much for a prolonged stay. People in safe areas with a spare room were urged to take in evacuees. They would be paid 10/6d a week for the first child and 8/6d for each subsequent child – certainly an incentive for low income families.

My sister loved her new uniform and her new school, but we both hated our billet lady. I decided that, although the Chief Rabbi had said we could eat *traife* (not Kosher and not to be eaten by Jews) food in wartime, I wouldn't eat meat and I didn't like much else. I lost weight and my father finally took us home just before Christmas.

This was the time of the 'phony' war and many children had dribbled back to London. All the schools had been evacuated and were closed, but a temporary junior school was opened in Toynbee Hall where I could go. There were no grammar schools available, so my sister, who was nearly 14, left school – so putting paid to her hopes of becoming a doctor.

I vowed I would never be evacuated again but when the Blitz started in September 1940 I was sent to Dawlish, South Devon and stayed there for two years. My parents and sisters were like strangers when I came back to London in 1942.

My sister loved her new school uniform – especially that velour hat.

14. BEVIS MARKS SYNAGOGUE LONDON EC3

My dad was born in England but his parents came from Poland and my mother emigrated to the UK from Belarus in 1903, so we were Ashkenazi Jews (Jews who came from eastern Europe). We lived in Petticoat Lane and our local *shul* (synagogue) was the fabulous Great Synagogue in Duke's Place, until it was bombed in 1941. A one-storey pre-fab was soon erected on the bomb site and I preferred it, though it was just a concrete box. Now instead of the women being upstairs behind a railing, we sat in the centre with the men on either side. Much easier to catch the eye of a boyfriend and indicate it was time to take a 'break'.

I'd heard of Bevis Marks Synagogue, of course, but there was such a divide between Ashkenazi and Sephardi Jews (Jews from *Sepharad* – Spain and Portugal) that it wasn't until last year that I visited it. Built in 1701, it is the only *shul* in Europe to have held regular services continuously for over 300 years.

Sephardic Jews were finally allowed by Cromwell into the UK in the 17th century, long after Isabella of Castile and Fernando II of Aragon expelled the Jews in 1492 (the *Decreto de la Alhambra*). Being established here so long, they included some of the wealthiest Jewish families. I was expecting something magnificent – even grander than my childhood memories of the Great Synagogue. Instead I found a small *shul*, peaceful and calm, with a strong sense of piety. It had none of the grandeur of my <u>shul</u>. The ladies' section was up a small old twisting staircase.

It was still an incredible experience.

The entrance to Bevis Marks Synagogue

15. WHITECHAPEL PUBLIC LIBRARY -1892-2005

For me Whitechapel Library was a godsend. The only books our family owned were six *Sidurim* (Daily Prayer Books) and six *Haggadahs* (Prayer Books for the first two nights of *Pesach* - Passover). - one each for my grandmother, my parents, my two older sisters and me. No reading books. Those we borrowed from the library.

I could already read when I was enrolled at Jews Free Infant School aged 3, but I couldn't join the children's section of Whitechapel Library until I was five. From then on, I went to the library every Friday afternoon before the Sabbath began. Hard to believe in our apparently more dangerous age, but I went there on my own as soon as I was old enough to join, walking from our tenement in Wentworth Dwellings, crossing the busy Commercial Street, walking up Old Montague Street and cutting through to the Library.

My mother would tell me to find a big man to take me across Commercial Street and to hold his hand tight. These days parents would fear that the 'big man' was a paedophile or worse.

I could borrow six books a week from the Children's section and later, when I was old enough, from the Adult Library, so for me most of the titles in *'1000 Books You Must Read before You Die'* are familiar, even if I've only skimmed them - though most I'd have read cover to cover. As an Orthodox Jewish girl there was little else I could do on Saturdays after getting back from *shul* and having lunch.

There was a plaque at the bottom of the staircase to J. Passmore Edwards in recognition of the philanthropist's substantial contribution to its construction under the aegis of Canon Samuel Barnett and his wife Henrietta. It was only when looking at the photograph of the library that I first saw the inscription on the building 'The Passmore Edwards Library'. I never heard anyone call it that.

The only thing I hated about the library was walking past the cases of stuffed animals and birds, if I needed to look up something in the Reference Library upstairs. I can still picture the glaring eyes and sharp teeth of the foxes and visualise the poor little songbirds tied to twigs.

I'm sure the new Ideas Store further up Whitechapel Road that replaced it after it was closed as a library in 2005 does a great job, but it's nothing like the glorious old Whitechapel Library of my memories.

Whitechapel Library and an entrance to Aldgate East underground

16. THE BLITZ AND RE-EVACUATION 1940-1942

When my dad brought my middle sister and me back from an unhappy billet in Ely, Christmas 1939, I vowed I would never be evacuated again, but on September 7th 1940 the *Blitz* began. We tried taking shelter on the platform of Aldgate East Underground station, where we slept in rows tightly packed like sardines. I hated it there. I often walked in my sleep and, although I knew that the electric current was turned off at night, I was terrified that I might walk to the edge of the platform and fall onto the lines. Finally, we were allocated spaces in the basement of a factory in Middlesex Street and started to sleep there every night.

Soon, posters appeared saying that children still in London should be sent to the country. I told my parents I wouldn't go. After the miserable time I'd had in Ely, I absolutely didn't want to be evacuated again but a distant cousin was working at one of the hostels for Jewish children opened by *Habonim* (a Jewish Youth Movement) in South Devon – one each in Dawlish, Teignmouth and Exmouth. There was room for me in the Dawlish hostel and I stayed there for two years, finally coming back to London in the summer of 1942.

I loved it there. I was the youngest and smallest and for the first time I wasn't just a third unwelcome daughter, but was cossetted and made a big fuss of. And there were lots of children to play with. I don't remember ever being homesick even though I only saw my parents a couple of times in the two years I was there – it was a long way from London and the fare was expensive. I wasn't exactly alienated from my family but certainly there was now an emotional as well as a geographical distance.

I was entered for the Junior County Scholarship when I was 10 and awarded a scholarship to Christ's Hospital. I'd read lots of books about boarding schools and couldn't wait to go there, but my father wrote to the school asking if I would be able to take Jewish holydays off. Needless to say, the reply was that no special arrangements could be made for Jewish children and my Orthodox parents wouldn't allow me to go there.

I was heartbroken and now I hated the hostel and begged my father to take me home. My scholarship didn't guarantee me a free place at the local grammar school, Central Foundation School for Girls, but the headmistress allowed me to go there free of charge provided I won a Junior County Scholarship the following spring. It was a fee-paying school at the time, and my parents wouldn't have been able to afford to pay fees. Fortunately, with a bit of taking in, my middle sister's uniform fitted me, so my parents were spared that expense.

I won a Junior County scholarship in 1943 and spent seven happy years at CFS, including the last two as the only girl at our brother school – Cowper Street Boys School – but that's another story!!

Dawlish 1941

17. THE ONLY GIRL IN THE BOYS' SCHOOL

There was a shortage of teachers at Higher School Certificate (A level) standard in 1947, the year I went into the VIth form. Some had not yet been demobbed and some had left the profession. Too many had been killed in action. Several schools solved the problem by combining sixth forms. Our school, Central Foundation School for Girls, combined sixth forms with our brother school, Central Foundation School for Boys (Cowper Street School). The boys would take Arts subjects at our school and we would take Physics, Botany and Zoology at the boys' school. Our own chemistry teacher could teach to A level standard.

I originally wanted to become a teacher, but my mother put me off. 'You'll never get married,' she said. 'They're all old maids, the lot of them.' In those days, whatever we wanted to do with our lives, we girls were heavily indoctrinated with the idea that to be a 'proper' woman we had to get married and have children. My mother didn't know about the Marriage Bar for Female Teachers. It wasn't abolished until 1935, so some of our teachers were old enough to have been caught in its trap. If a women teacher wanted to get married, she had to leave or, as some did, get married secretly. So all women teachers were spinsters – or seemed to be!

I decided I'd become a doctor. I have to admit that I was partly influenced by the fact that to study medicine I'd need Physics, Zoology, Botany and Chemistry at A level and that I'd need to go to the boys' school for the first three. Surely amongst 500 boys there'd be some dishy ones.

I was the only girl taking Science at the boys' school that year or the next. On my first day, I arrived at the end of morning break. At our school, we queued one behind the other to go back after break, but the boys lined up side-by-side. All 500 stood facing my path to the Science block. The scruffiest, spottiest, first years at the front kept up a muted barrage of personal remarks and wolf whistles, until a master strode over and knocked two of their heads together. I had no idea there were so many spotty boys around. Where had all the good-looking ones gone?

The physics master tried his best with me, but I found physics baffling and it took me months to catch up with the boys. They'd been playing with electrical sets and motors for years.

But I did manage to come top of all three subjects at the end of the first year. The headmaster wasn't pleased to have to award the Cowper Street Boys' School prizes to a girl.

The Boys' School Badge

18. HAPPY BIRTHDAY BABE

When your younger son is 57 today and his elder brother is 59 you realise you really are old!!

When our elder son, Simon, was in nappies we had those terry towelling napkins you had to soak and wash daily. By the time Bernard was born, disposable nappies were available and the make we used was called 'Golden Babe.' Unlike the rest of our family, Bernard had white-gold hair and his nickname was soon 'Golden Babe' or 'Babe' for short.

Simon was three and Bernard was 6 months old when we moved them out of the box room and into a junior bed and larger cot in the spare bedroom. To our horror, the first morning the boys were in their new bedroom, Simon scribbled all over one newly painted wall. 'Why did you do that?' We asked. He looked over at Babe, who had just learned to sit up alone, and certainly hadn't yet started to speak. 'Well,' he said. 'Babe and me thought it was a good idea.'

We couldn't be cross. It was such a great saying!! Now 'Babe and me thought it was a good idea' is our family saying for when someone does something unexpected and stupid.

The following year we opened our educational toy shop, John Dobbie, in Wimbledon Village and amongst our stock we sold fancy dress clothes. They both loved dressing up.

The boys in dressing-up clothes

19. *KOL NIDREI* AT THE GREAT SYNAGOGUE, DUKES PLACE

Being Ashkenazi and living in Petticoat Lane, we went to The Great Synagogue in Dukes Place rather than the Sephardi *shul*, Bevis Marks, about the same distance away. I remember always arriving after the Shabbat or Yom Tov services had begun, pushing past the knees of the ladies in the Ladies' Gallery upstairs and looking down at the men seated below. My memories are of illustrations of the 12 tribes of Israel in the windows and wondering to which tribe I would have belonged. I knew I wasn't an aristocratic Levy or a Cohen. However, all the photographs of the *shul* before it was bombed in 1942 show plain glass. Maybe I am confusing it with somewhere else., but I definitely remember the magnificent chandeliers.

When I came back from being evacuated to Dawlish in the summer of 1942, the *shul* had been destroyed and we went to services at Toynbee Hall until a single story building was erected on the Dukes Place site in 1943. I much preferred it. Instead of being upstairs and quite separate from the men - and any boys of my age - we were at the same level, with the women in the centre and the men on either side.

My father was a paid-up member so we always had reserved seats. On *Erev Yom Kippur* (the evening before the day of Atonement when the holyday and the fast begin) the *shul* was full to bursting, with people standing in the gangways and some standing outside, straining to hear the *Kol Nidrei* (Aramaic for 'All vows') sung by Simcha Koussevitzky. What an incredible sound!! Many were in tears, had already lost loved ones in the war. Others were refugees, weeping for their lost homeland. It was an amazing experience.

Next day was a bit of a bore. Mainly praying, fasting, getting more and more hungry, and little singing. Though I could read Hebrew, I couldn't understand much of it and I had read the side-by-side English translation many times. Catching the eye of a boy at the side, we would slip out ostensibly for *Tachlich* - walking to the Tower of London to wash away our sins in the River Thames. Time for a quick cuddle at home in those more innocent times and then back to the odiferous breaths of all those fasting from the evening before. Finally, a delicious meal to break the fast.

The Great Synagogue before it was bombed in 1942 - the men downstairs and the ladies up in the gallery (from Ackerman's *Microcosm of London*)

20. I REMEMBER, I REMEMBER

Amongst my most powerful memories of living in Petticoat Lane are the smells. I make my own bread and when I smell baking I'm taken back to our cold water tenement in Wentworth Dwellings.

From 1943 we lived on the third floor with my bedroom facing on to Wentworth Street and Kossoff's bakery. The smell when I woke first thing in the morning was delicious – it made me ravenous. Then there were the aromas of pickled cucumbers and pickled herrings from the barrels outside Marks, the delicatessen. I don't like schmaltz (pickled in brine) or chopped herrings - but I love the pickled onions that come with them. In a sandwich of rye bread still warm from the baker, they are heaven.

My bedroom was above the hardware shop with its odours of carbolic acid and paraffin. I was often sent down to buy a packet of flypapers – sticky yellow curls of stiff paper that you hang up and wait for flies to attach themselves. When it's completely covered with dead and dying flies you hang up another – but there were always more around in those pre-fridge days.

Bed bugs were a constant problem. We tried Flit sprays and pouring white spirit over the bed springs, but neither did much good. The springs were attached to the headboards by tightly curled wires in which bed bugs made their home. My mother would regularly pour boiling water over them but they always came back. When the war ended in 1945, we were visited by council workers with DDT sprays that did the trick – at least for a time. We didn't know then that DDT was dangerous - for humans as well as for bedbugs.

Earlier, my family had lived in a smaller Wentworth Dwellings flat, this time facing onto Goulston Street. On our side of the road were the chicken stalls with crates of live chickens clucking underneath. On the other side, by Brunswick Dwellings, were the fish stalls. The fish was always fresh that day - collected from Billingsgate Market as soon as it was light - but the fish heads and bits and pieces chucked away under the stalls made that side of the road really smelly. I can still conjure up that whiff of ammonia and hated walking on that side of the street. The discarded offal from the chicken stalls added their own aroma to the mix.

And then there were all the street cries. When my husband wants to tease me, he'll call out 'Ripe tomatoes, shilling a pound,' reminding me of my East End past. I'd rather he'd have chosen 'Sweet strawberries. Melt in your mouth.'

On Sundays, Petticoat Lane was quite different – much more crowded and spreading to all the surrounding streets. Now the hucksters were calling out their crockery and linen wares instead of fruit and vegetables. Completely different smells – now of leather and fabric.

If you were lucky, you might hear Prince Monolulu crying 'I gotta horse!!', the long ostrich feathers in his headdress and his chieftain's fly whisk waving in the breeze. They said he'd won what was then the vast sum of £8000 in the Derby in 1920. It brought you luck to touch or even be near him.

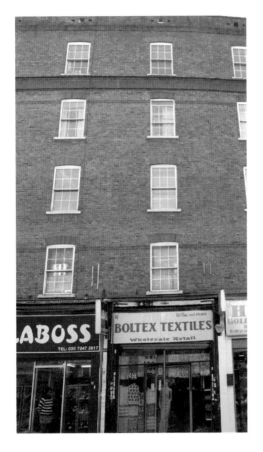

Our 3rd floor flat facing Wentworth Street

21. I MANAGED TO TURN 88 TODAY

I have survived being in London in WW2 in the Blitz, and when Doodlebugs and V2 rockets were falling, a near-fatal heart attack, breast cancer, several broken bones and a slew of quite serious medical conditions. Perhaps it was having the same loving husband for the last 64 years and four fantastic children!!

I look back to a time when we could play cricket in Wentworth Street after the market closed. We'd scour the fruiterers' refuse for a clean orange box that would provide both the wicket and the bat, hoping we wouldn't miss a nasty smelly surprise of a rotten green orange in a corner that our rushed inspection had missed. Cars were few and far between, even in Commercial Street, and none ventured down Petticoat Lane – except to deliver goods before the Sunday market opened. The everyday demountable food stalls arrived on barrows. The sound as they trundled along first thing in the morning accompanied the smell of bread baking from Kossoff's bakery.

None of us had our own phones – an emergency sent someone running to the phone box outside Aldgate East station. You phoned your current boyfriend there– getting an hour's worth for a couple of pence. Now you can hardly walk along the pavement without bumping into someone too busy on their mobile to avoid bumping into you.

Of course, they weren't all good old days. My dad was out of work in the Great Depression. Not sure how we scraped by. And without our fantastic NHS and immunisation, we children all got measles, or mumps, or chicken pox, or diphtheria or any combination of them.

We've so much to be grateful for that just wasn't available when I was a child.

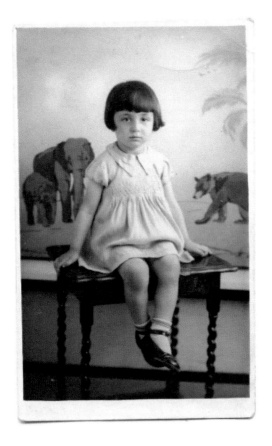

I look pretty serious in this photo of me from 1934. Perhaps I was pondering the future of mankind or how to save endangered elephants and bears!!

22. ON LOSING SOME OF MY MARBLES

I always agree with Edith Piaf when I hear a recording of her singing 'Je ne regrette rien', but it sounds so much more elegant than 'I regret nothing'!

I'm used to feeling a bit sorry for myself – coming from a poor family, being brought up in London's East End in a cold-water tenement infested with bed bugs and mice, probably a bit malnourished, dragged away from my family to be evacuated far from home, childhood illnesses, a string of adult accidents and illnesses etc.

But I am now re-reading David Eagleman's fascinating book 'The Brain'. According to him, all these experiences helped my brain to develop, forged new neural connections and put off the time I might finally lose my marbles.

I seemed to be doing fine after my heart attack. I had a couple of stents inserted to reopen my blocked coronary arteries, but then I deteriorated and needed to have an intra-aortic heart pump and be put on a ventilator. When I came off those and off the heavy sedation, not only did I have a series of weird hallucinations and delusions, but often I couldn't think of the word for something (*nominal aphasia*). That's gradually improved, though I think 'It's on the tip of my tongue' more often than before my coronary. It makes me feel better when someone much younger than me says they can't think of the exact word they're after.

At 88, I no longer have the photographic memory that helped me through my exams, but I am attending classes in Music and Art History, I have piano lessons and I am about to join a beginners' class in Classical Greek (PG).

I love being the oldest person in the class even though I may now be a penny short of a pound!!

I still have a cupful of real marbles

23. SOME VERY UNWELCOME VISITORS

It was the week before our end of year exams as final year medical students. They would cover medicine, surgery and obstetrics but meanwhile we had to keep up with looking after our patients on the ward. I was on a three month medical rotation and had a case to present on Grand Rounds the day after next.

I got down my medical textbook, changed into pyjamas and snuggled up next to Joshua. We'd found a furnished basement flat near the hospital and moved in when we returned from honeymoon. It was convenient but decidedly chilly, so bed was the best place to study.

I was in the middle of reading up liver disease, when something jumped onto my book and off again. I dug Josh in the ribs.

'Something jumped onto my book,' I said.

'You're imagining things. It's late. Go to sleep.'

But next evening, when I got to kidney disease, it happened again but, by the time I'd alerted Josh, it had vanished.

The following morning, I was packing my briefcase in the living room ready to go to the hospital when I felt something bite my ankle. To my horror, there were several tiny black things on my lower legs under my tights. I rolled down my tights and brushed them off and hurried off to my ward round. I was terrified that I'd missed one of the wretched things and that it would jump out while I was presenting my case. My consultant had a particularly sharp tongue.

'We brought one of our little friends with us, did we Miss Waterman?', he would say, sarcastic as ever.

Luckily, I was spared that embarrassment and as soon as I got home phoned the local Pest Control Officer.

'It sounds as if you've got cat fleas, miss. Do you have a cat?'

I'd been upset enough before and now I was in tears.

'We think he must have been run over by a car. Rupert crawled home but died soon after.'

'Sorry to hear that miss. Do you have carpets where you live?'

Our landlord had left a large beige shag carpet in the living room.

'That's it then. Some eggs must have been left there and hatched out. Cat fleas prefer cats but they'll also feed off humans. They go for pale areas like your ankles. But don't worry they'll drop off.'

'Will you come and spray or something?'

'No need. Just be patient. They won't go on breeding.'

We hoovered the carpet a million times and I made Josh inspect my legs each morning before I left for the hospital. Fortunately, we never saw another flea.

I looked up cat fleas. They can jump vertically up to 7" (18 cm) and horizontally up to 13" (33cm) making them one of the best jumping animals after the froghopper. Jumping onto my medical textbooks or my ankles was a breeze for such an athletic beast.

Our gorgeous tabby Rupert 1958

24. SPITALFIELDS FRUIT AND VEGETABLE MARKET AND CLASSICAL GREEK

What's the connection? The connection is Latin.

I would hurry through the old Spitalfields Fruit and Vegetable market to my school in Spital Square, Central Foundation School for Girls, avoiding the squashed fruit and vegetables that had fallen off the lorries and the piles of horse droppings, repeating to myself the Latin vocabulary we'd had to learn for that morning. At our school, the choice was Latin or German. The top stream did Latin and that was that.

We had a fantastic Latin mistress, Irish, fierce, with bright red hair and a sense of humour that kept us in fits of laughter. I could take or leave what Caesar had to say about his Gallic Wars and in those more innocent times I wasn't quite sure what Dido and Aeneas were up to in the cave, but I loved the preciseness and predictability of Latin.

Latin was later useful to me when I came to study medicine, helping to interpret the names of tissues and diseases. But many more names of diseases were derived from Greek – not on offer at our school.

I'd been thinking about taking Classical Greek after I retired and I enrolled for a class in a Further Education College, but my near-fatal heart attack got in the way. Now four years later, age 88, I am about to start Classical Greek Level 1.

Wish me luck!!

Our Greek textbooks

25. STREET GAMES IN PETTICOAT LANE

After the stallholders packed up, and the dustman cleared their rubbish away, Wentworth Street was ours. We didn't have to worry about traffic. We never saw a vehicle other than a dustcart in Wentworth Street and I was a teenager before I saw a boy rich enough to ride into our patch on a bicycle, albeit one that was chipped and with a couple of spokes missing.

We'd bring down an old tennis ball, rescue a clean orange box to make a wicket and bat to play cricket, or an old can for 'Tin Can Tommy'. These were the games we played in Wentworth Street itself.

Others were played in the courtyard between the three blocks that comprised Wentworth Dwellings. A supply of chalk nicked from school while the teacher's back was turned was essential for drawing the double and single squares of Hopscotch, and for the Spiral, whose purpose I've forgotten. We always played our skipping games in the courtyard rather than in the street. There were waist-high railings above the basements where the big, odiferous dustbins loitered with their menagerie of rats, mice, and feral cats. We would tie one end of the rope to the railings and then only one girl – and it was only girls who skipped – would need to hold the other end. The rest of us would join in the current skipping game one by one.

Even more enjoyable was 'Knock Down Ginger'. We would run up and down the staircases lifting the heavy U-shaped iron knockers high and letting them go with a bang. If you were lucky a woman would come to the door still in curlers and a petticoat, or a man in his underwear, shaking his fist at you if you hadn't yet disappeared around the corner.

The flats in the central block didn't have their own toilets. There were two pairs of back-to back loos in the centre of the long corridor that connected the flats on each floor. They only had a black latch to close them, and the door was just too far away to hold it shut while you sat on the toilet. It was fun catching grown-ups with their trousers or knickers down, except if it was Polly's father. He'd threaten terrible revenge if you disturbed him reading the paper or having a quick fag while enthroned.

Behind the Sainsbury Wing of the National Gallery is a short street with a row of bollards on the pavement on one side to stop you parking. They would have been perfect for leap-frog. We'd have loved to race along, up and over them, when we'd tired of leaping over each other. We didn't have those big domed litter bins. They too would have been fair game for us too.

Happy days!!

Bollards and a litter bin behind the Sainsbury's Wing

26. 1944 AND WW2 IS DRAGGING ON

Hitler was still sending nightly bombing sorties against London so we slept in our designated shelter, the converted basement of a factory in Middlesex Street. The authorities had installed black metal bunk beds, as well as lockers and chemical toilets against one wall. I would gather up my most precious possessions – my pressed flower book from the Holy Land, my best cardigan and the place mats I was embroidering - and stuff them into a pillowcase, together with my homework and a torch, so I could read under the blankets after the main lights were turned off.

We children expected to get one or more childhood fevers. I caught measles, chicken pox, rubella and whooping cough in turn. That was about par for the course. I was left with a cough for years and a few little pock marks on my face, but I was lucky - there was a significant mortality associated with these infections. Some children were left blind or deaf from measles and every school had children wearing leg braces to support limbs damaged by polio. The only immunisation/ vaccination we had was against smallpox.

The last infectious disease I caught was Scarlet Fever and I loved having it.

As I trailed after my mother to the shelter, I was feeling worse and worse. My head ached and my throat was sore. By next morning, my chest was covered in a vivid red rash.

I don't remember at which stage I saw a doctor, but I was soon wrapped in a soft red blanket and packed off in an ambulance to Hither Green Isolation Hospital - Scarlet Fever is very infectious. It was so exciting. I'd never been in an ambulance before. I loved it when they turned on the bell when they couldn't get through traffic.

At the hospital, the examining doctor congratulated me. He said I had the classical Strawberry Tongue of Scarlet Fever and bemoaned the fact there were no medical students to admire it. The nurses took my clothes away to be fumigated and I was admitted to a ward full of crying toddlers and babies.

Antibiotics weren't yet available so I just had to wait for the disease to take its course. After a couple of days, I felt fine. Fortunately, there was one girl of my age, Ellie. There were separate one storey buildings for each infectious disease, set in quite extensive grounds. Ellie and I could wander at will. The wards were called by different letters and each had a tree planted nearby whose name began with that letter. Being in Q ward, I met quinces for the first time.

It was lovely having a friend of my own age and wonderful not having to sleep in a crowded shelter, nor having to use the smelly chemical toilets. But while I was in hospital, Hitler started to send over Doodlebugs, unmanned explosive planes which didn't have to wait for the cover of darkness to avoid anti-aircraft fire and could be sent over day or night.

I think I was in hospital about 2 weeks. The good thing was that when I was discharged home, there was now no point in sleeping in the shelter that I hated. I could sleep in my own bed, curled up in my lovely feather 'parana' - bed bugs and all!!

Hither Green Scarlet Fever Hospital was opened 1897 and after being used for a number of different medical specialities, it was closed in 1997. It was designed by Edwin Thomas Hall, who also designed the Liberty Stores in Regent Street. The hospital has been demolished and the site is now a housing complex, Meridian South.

From *Lost Hospitals of London*

27. MY RUSSIAN BUBBA

My two older sisters and I adored our maternal grandmother. She lived with us in our cold water tenement in Wentworth Dwellings in Petticoat Lane until she died in 1937, when I was five and my sisters 11 and 17. We were broken-hearted. It took years before it stopped hurting.

There were six of us - my parents, my bubba, my two sisters and me. The flat had three rooms - a bedroom, living room and kitchen, together with a small balcony which had a coal bunker and outside toilet. My parents shared the bedroom, my sisters, my grandmother and I slept in the 'living room', while the tiny kitchen was where we sat around a small oilcloth-covered table, talked, read, cooked and washed at the china butler sink. There was only a cold tap, so water for washing or when we were little for the zinc bath, was heated in a kettle on the black iron stove-cum -fireplace. My sisters shared a pull-out sofa while I slept with my grandmother in the large mahogany double bed that had been my parents' until they changed to the more modern twin beds. The living room was freezing in the winter - fern-like Jack Frost etched on the windowpanes - so it was lovely curling up against my grandmother's warm back.

The outside loo had a long heavy iron chain with a wooden pull. The noise terrified me if I had to have a pee in the night. I don't remember how old I was when it became my task to tear my dad's newspaper into neat squares after he'd read it cover-to-cover. He'd then force through a nail and thread some string through to hang the bundle by. There was no question of wasting money on bought toilet paper, but even when my sisters left home, and we were a bit better off, my dad preferred his newspaper to the bought stuff my mother and I used.

My *bubba* was a tall commanding woman, with dark hair piled on top of her head. It would have been a *sheitel* – the wig orthodox married women wear over their shaved head. I never saw her without it. Her left eye was badly scarred. It had been pieced by a shard of glass when the Cossacks came riding through her village, pillaging and looting.

My mother and grandmother came from Mogilev in Belarus. My maternal grandfather died when my mother was only 2 years old, so my grandmother scraped a living turning her tiny cottage into a lodging house. The lodgers slept on a circular shelf around the pot-bellied stove in the centre of the room and ate at the table my grandfather had made my *bubba* as a wedding present. My father's parents had died long before I was born.

I'm not sure whether my grandmother could speak Russian - she always spoke Yiddish to us and we replied in English. My mother could read and write Russian, so she kept the accounts required by the Russian authorities. They emigrated to England in about 1903 and lived on the pittance my grandmother earned selling beigels on the corner of Wentworth Street and Goulston Street. My mother was apprenticed aged eleven to a dressmaker, earning 3d a week. Once she had learned enough to be useful, her employer stopped using her as a cheap servant and paid her a small wage. However, my grandmother refused to give up her pitch until my parents got married in 1918 and moved to Old Kent Road.

My bubba always did more than her fair share of the housework. She had a stroke while cleaning the stone steps leading down to the next landing. She was dead on arrival at the London Hospital. The neighbours blamed my mother.

'Fancy letting her clean the stairs at her age, and her half-blind,' they said.

But there was no stopping my grandmother doing anything she'd decided on.

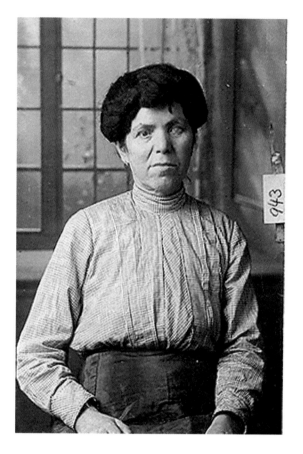

My maternal grandmother in clothes my mother made for her

28. THE KINDNESS OF A STRANGER

Nowadays having lice is almost a badge of honour. I realised this when my very upper crust neighbour rang the bell to tell me that her daughter Fiona had lice, and that I should check my four for the nasty little things. She sounded quite proud of the fact. So different from when I was a child. Then if you had lice, it meant that you were poor, came from a dirty home and probably your mother didn't love you. Same parasites - different time and different attitude.

It was Sophie who noticed the navy blue suited figure crossing the playground.

'It's Nitty Nora,' she hissed, loudly enough for the whole class to hear.

The Health Visitor called at our school on a regular basis, checking for lice and scabies. Our form mistress, Miss Evans, came to our classroom at the end of Latin.

'Make your way to the First Aid room, girls, and line up in alphabetical order. Behave yourselves now. You don't want to make me ashamed of you.'

I was last but one - Waterman came before Zaperstein.

'Hold out your hands,' the Health Visitor directed. 'I'm pleased to see at least one girl has got nice clean nails,' she said, as she inspected my hands for the tell-tale burrows of scabies.

She went on to look through my hair, especially in the warm places behind my ears, and then dismissed me.

Miss Evans stopped me as I queued to leave at the end of the afternoon and handed me a small brown envelope. You used to be able to steam those envelopes open and be forewarned about any wrongdoing on your part, but the teachers now sealed the envelopes with a strip of sellotape.

I held my breath as my mother opened it.

Dear Mrs Waterman

This is to inform you that your daughter Abigail Waterman has been found to be infested with lice. You are required to take her to Finsbury Square Cleansing station at 8am tomorrow morning. She will be unable to attend school until she is certified free of lice and nits.

My mother was furious.

'You insisted on washing your hair yourself and now look at the state of you - lice indeed. You've disgraced me and disgraced our family. They'll think I'm a bad mother.'

She insisted on washing my hair twice that evening and there was certainly no supper that day.

I went on my own to the Cleansing Station, sitting as far as possible from anyone else on the bus lest they see lice crawling through my hair. I stood at the top of the stairs leading down to a mahogany door with a porthole in it filled with pebbled glass. The brass handrail gleamed in the winter sunlight as did the fittings on the door.

Instead of the ogre I was expecting, a jolly plump red-faced woman opened the door wide, a beaming smile on her face.

'Come on in, my dear. I don't bite.'

She washed my hair twice with anti-lice shampoo that smelled strongly of carbolic and combed it with a toothcomb. Towelling it almost dry, she sat me down in front of the fire with a sweet cup of tea and a biscuit.

'Don't be upset, sweetheart,' she said. 'I get plenty of clean girls through my hands. Anyone can catch the horrid little things. I'm afraid you can't go back to school today, my love. You need to come back tomorrow and if there are no lice or nits left, I'll give you a note saying that you are free of them.'

I felt like kissing her, but I was too shy.

No-one at school seemed to know or care why I had been away for a day and I never had lice again as a child. It wasn't until I had four louse-ridden children that I caught head lice again - but that's another story.

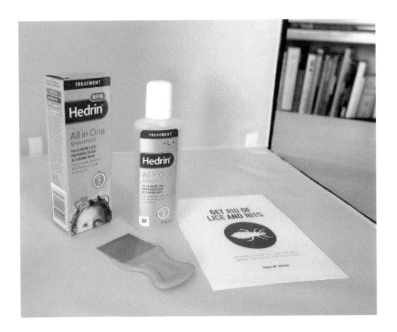

I'm not sure whether solutions like this were available then.

29. FRIDAY NIGHTS IN PETTICOAT LANE

I loved Friday nights. My middle sister Hannah and I would sit in the kitchen sparkling clean, as my mother placed a scarf over her head, lit the four candles and intoned the Sabbath blessing. She always lit the candles in the brass candlesticks first. They were the ones she'd bought with her own money long before she got married. The silver ones were a present from my father's wealthier parents and not nearly as precious.

Except in the depths of winter, when the Sabbath came in too early for there to be time between the end of school and the beginning of the Sabbath, my mother would take Hannah and me up the road to Goulston Street baths. She would buy just one second class ticket and bathe my sister and me together. We would then wait on the polished wooden bench in the corridor outside, while she called for more hot water and had her bath. The attendants bustled past in their immaculate white overalls, holding their badge of office – the big brass key that controlled the flow of water into the big porcelain baths. It was only in the First Class baths that you had your own taps and could control your own bath water.

My mother didn't wash our hair in the bath. She was sure that walking the couple of hundred yards home to our tenement in Wentworth Dwellings would result in a cold or worse. She'd wash our hair over the sink when we got home, heating kettles of water on the stove.

When my father got home from synagogue he would lift the embroidered cloth covering the *challah* (plaited loaf), say the *brochas* (blessings) for wine and bread and pass around the *kiddush* (blessing over wine) cup for a sip each and a piece of the poppy sprinkled bread. Supper was always cold fried fish, potato salad and home-made *chrane* – a fiery mixture of grated beetroot and horseradish. We tried to make it last as long as possible. Nothing like grating horseradish root to make your eyes stream.

After supper, we all had something to say as we sat around the table. We sisters had to take turns. When I thought no-one was looking, I would pick some warm wax drips from the candles and roll them in my fingers under the tablecloth. If she caught me, my older sister, Rebecca. would smack my hand and hiss 'They're the *Shabbat* (sabbath) candles. Mustn't touch.'

The only bad thing about Friday night is that I had to go to bed in the dark – it was forbidden to carry out any work on the Sabbath - switching on a light was considered work. I would pray not to have to go to the loo in the dark. The long clanking chain made me think of ghosts hauling their shackles behind them and I'd scuttle there and back as fast as I could.

Hannah, my middle sister, went to bed early too. She would offer to tell me a story. It was always a ghost story, that nearly frightened the life out of me. Then she would say that her name was Cynthia Levy and that she had trapped my sister, who I loved dearly, in the light bulb. Unless I did everything she ordered me to do, she would whip Hannah until she bled. It meant me doing things like switching the light on and off – though it was forbidden – and crawling under my bed amongst all the dust bunnies. I'd finally be allowed to creep under my *parana* (feather-filled duvet) - Hannah now saved from the light bulb.

In spite of 'Cynthia Levy' I still miss those magical Friday nights.

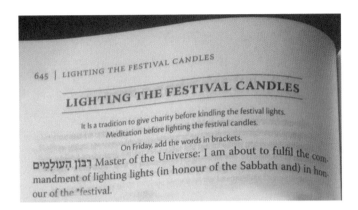

LIGHTING THE FESTIVAL CANDLES

It is a tradition to give charity before kindling the festival lights.
Meditation before lighting the festival candles.
On Friday, add the words in brackets.

רִבּוֹן הָעוֹלָמִים Master of the Universe: I am about to fulfil the commandment of lighting lights (in honour of the Sabbath and) in honour of the *festival.

Before lighting the candles, one should give to charity and meditate

30. OFF TO THE USA

As far as the *shadchen* (matchmaker) was concerned, my mother was no *matseer* (bargain). She was pretty enough, and a capable dressmaker who could earn her own living, but she was a fatherless girl and lived with her widowed half-blind mother, who would have to be part of any new household. She'd hardly known her father. He died in Russia when she was only two years old. He'd made a living carrying sacks of ice on his back to deliver to the rich; caught pneumonia and died. There was certainly no dowry on offer.

Then my mother met Harry at a *kiddush* - the blessing for wine but also the ceremony where blessing is said and refreshments taken) after a Saturday service.

A personable young man, he was an accomplished tailor who had decided to emigrate to America. They were soon making marriage plans, but he was determined to make his way in the USA before getting married. He left a couple of months after they met and promised to send for my mother and grandmother when he had found a job and somewhere for them all to live. My mother started making her trousseau - silk blouses, tweed and plain skirts, lacy nightdresses, a silk negligee.

He wrote to say he was now settled in and to come. My mother was to go to America first and send for my grandmother later. She took the train to Liverpool and boarded the ship for New York and Ellis Island. She was surprised and put off, when Harry came to meet her with the daughter of the boss of the factory where he worked on his arm. He assured my mother that they were just friends, found her a room in a nearby lodging house and a job with a young dressmaker making her way in the new country.

By the time she sent for my grandmother, my mother was suspicious of Harry's intentions but she sent the ticket money just the same. It was not to be. By law, there had to be a doctor on boats carrying emigrants to check that they were healthy and didn't carry any communicable diseases. When the doctor examined my grandmother, he misdiagnosed her scarred eye and cataracts as trachoma – a highly infectious eye disease - and refused to allow her passage.

Harry said he couldn't help himself; he'd fallen in love. Broken-hearted my mother booked a passage home, but at least she could tell everyone she had come home because her mother couldn't follow her. She needn't admit that she'd been jilted.

By this time, the shadchen had persuaded my father, one of seven sons of a wealthy family, that my mother was a worthy wife for him. She hadn't got over Harry, but my mother thought at least she was marrying a rich man. She didn't know that he had gambled away his inheritance, nor that he was saddled with taking care of his younger brother. They married in 1918 and moved to Old Kent Road with my grandmother and uncle, and opened a Newsagent and Tobacconist shop there.

Harry came back to the UK when my elder sister was 2 years old. He begged my mother to go back to the USA with him. His marriage had been a terrible mistake and he would divorce his harridan of a wife.

But my mother wouldn't leave my grandmother once more and they never met again.

My mother (at the back) with friends and one of their daughters just before she left for the USA

31. THE PETTICOAT LANE EXPERIENCE

I was thinking about all the skills that were needed when I lived in Petticoat Lane 1931-1956.

From 1938 until September 1939, when WW2 was declared and we were evacuated to Ely, every weekday I walked down Bell Lane on my way to Jews Free Junior School in Frying Pan Alley. Then 1942-1949, I walked on through Spitalfields Fruit and Vegetable Market to Central Foundation School for Girls in Spital Square. At the beginning of Bell Lane there were shops and houses with wooden doors that were regularly repainted. I would watch as the painter rubbed down the old paint then applied a pale coat and let it dry. He'd paint the door with brown varnish and draw a comb though the wet varnish, creating intricate patterns of wood grain and knots. He was a real artist.

The porters in Spitalfields Market could carry a tower of 5 or 6 circular baskets of produce without dropping even a leaf while the fruit and vegetable stall holders in Wentworth Street created works of art out of the produce they carefully polished.

The itinerant tradesmen included the knife grinder who had a large stone wheel attached to his bicycle. Scissors were the most expensive to sharpen. If you brought him a pair he'd let you have a go sitting on the saddle. The chimney sweep appeared at the beginning of winter. We'd clear everything away from the fireplaces and cover the floor in front with old sheets. He'd screw together tube after tube and finally the circular brush. A few brisk twists up the chimney and out would come a load of soot. Quite often there would be a few feathers from the pigeons that roosted on the chimneys and occasionally a dead bird.

The coal man called all year round as we cooked and heated water on the black iron range. He'd come up to us on the third floor carrying a hundred weight sack of coal on his back, hardly breathless at all.

We cooked with enamel saucepans that were liable to develop holes where the vertical sides met the bottom. You could buy tin washers to screw in place, but that was a temporary measure. When the tinkers' caravan appeared, we took down our saucepans to be repaired properly.

Few grocery items came ready wrapped. The assistant would carve off a lump of butter, slap its sides with wooden paddles until it was a neat brick and wrap it in grease-proof paper. On getting it home, the butter would be placed in a saucer of cold water and covered with a damp muslin cloth whose ends dipped in the water. Evaporation of the water kept the butter cool. We had a small wooden cupboard on top of the coal bunker on our balcony, its sides enclosed with metal mesh. The butter was stored there as were bottles of milk, but after a day the milk had often turned sour. My mother drained it through a muslin cloth and made cream cheese with it.

The grocers dispensed loose products like granulated sugar and tea in paper funnels. The paper would be folded into a double square, then a triangle, opened and the point rolled tightly to seal it and the goods poured in. Salt came as a brick. We grated it as needed – mainly for making meat *Kosher*, getting rid of all the blood. Cube sugar came in packets, as did some biscuits, but there were always large square biscuit tins along the floor in front of the counter containing loose biscuits. One tin always contained broken biscuits - the cheapest of all and all too tempting to little thieving fingers

All those skills no longer needed!!

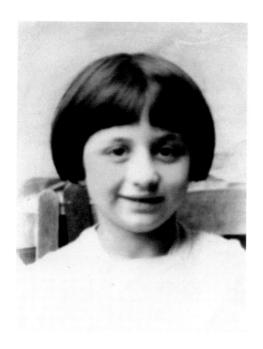

My school photo age 6

32. FISH AND CHIPS AND A BOTTLE OF TIZER

By the time WW2 was declared on September 3ʳᵈ 1939, over a million children had been evacuated from places deemed to be under threat. My middle sister, Hannah, had won a Supplementary Scholarship, which gave her a free grammar school place and uniform allowance, but she had not yet joined Central Foundation School for Girls, so she was evacuated with me from Jews Free School to Littleport in Cambridgeshire. We were first taken in by a farmer and his wife, but they decided having two children billeted on them was too much trouble. They forgot about us when they went to a wedding the next day and we were locked out until they came home late at night. The following day they offloaded us onto the farmer's mother who lived in Littleport village.

Mrs Hartley was a tiny, wrinkled old lady, her face all smiles. She kissed and hugged us both.

'Come in, come in, girls,' she said. 'So lovely to have children in the house again.'

Hers was a small two up/two down cottage with a pocket sized garden at the back and an outside toilet right at the end. The flowerbeds surrounding the weed-free lawn were ablaze with colour.

On the ground floor was a parlour that was hardly ever used and, at the back, a tiny kitchen with a small table, the three of us could just about fit around. Upstairs was Mrs Hartley's bedroom and a large double bedroom Hannah and I were to share.

'Now Mr Hartley has passed on, I don't need this large room,' she said.

There was a double bed with brass rails at either end and covered by a handmade patchwork quilt, a large mahogany wardrobe, a dressing table and stool, and a matching china basin and jug decorated with tiny pink roses. A flowered chamber pot peeped out from under the bed. We thought it was all gorgeous.

Mrs Hartley took us into the parlour and showed us a sepia photograph of a bearded Mr Hartley surrounded by three rows of children.

'Had 22,' she said. 'Raised 19,'

The rhyme 'The Old Woman Who Lived in a Shoe' came into my head. I couldn't imagine anyone having that many children, but I was sure she'd have loved them all.

Tea was fresh-from-the-oven, fruit scones with as much butter as we liked and home-made strawberry jam.

'Our old farm has a bathroom now, but it's a zinc bath in front of the kitchen fire for us,' she said.

I'd almost forgotten the rough feel of the ridges on a zinc bath, but the water was lovely and hot and the soap had a delicious flowery scent instead of the disinfectant-smelling Lifebuoy soap I was used to.

We went to bed early and cuddled up in the cosy, soft bed. Mrs Hartley had taken the chill off with a couple of stone hot water bottles.

We had a very special treat on Friday nights. Mrs Hartley would give us the money to buy three portions of fish and chips and a bottle of Tizer at the Fish and Chip shop up the road. At home we had only ever bought two penny worth of chips from Johnny Isaacs on our way home from the Troxy cinema. My mother cooked fried fish for Friday nights so we never bought any. The bright orange Tizer was new to us. As we ate, Hannah and I kept showing each other our tongues to see whose tongue was the brightest orange.

We loved staying with Mrs Hartley but Hannah's grammar school was evacuated to Ely. She and two other girls were bussed in each day while I went to the village school. The powers that be decided it was wasteful bussing in three CFS girls each day and Hannah and I were moved to a miserable billet on the outskirts of Ely.

I refused to eat the *traife* (non-kosher) meat the billet lady cooked, although the Chief Rabbi had said it was OK in Wartime, and I ate little of anything else. We were unhappy and I looked like a waif. We stuck it there until December 1939 and then my father brought us back to London.

Photograph of Littleport Village, probably from the 1900s. A resident
commented that it has changed very little. Such happy memories!!
With kind permission of the Littleport Society (littleportsociety.org.uk)

33. LITTLE WOMEN

It wasn't until my sister came to meet me at Tel Aviv airport that I realised
for the first time just how short I am. There was this little woman coming
towards me and, as she got nearer, I realised it was my sister, Hannah. We
hadn't seen each other for ages. She'd lived on a kibbutz since the late 1940s.
She came to London when I got married in 1956 and for a couple of visits
afterwards. As we kissed, I realised that she was a fraction taller than me – I
really had to be tiny!!

I do sometimes refer to myself jokingly as 'a little old woman', when I
want to boast about something or other – that at 88 I've not lost all my
marbles, for example. But my image of myself is not of a '5ft nothing' old
lady but of one at least 6 or 8 inches taller – until my two grandsons tower
over me as they kiss me *Hello* or *Goodbye*.

I didn't choose my best friends at school for that reason, but I realise now that they were all tiny too. This was not only due to our genes but, coming from poor families with mothers that did their best, we were probably underfed and undernourished as well. Certainly, we were all quite slender.

My mother was small too – though she seemed quite tall to me. Her wedding photographer was cunning. He put a box under the carpet where my mother stood, so the difference in height between my parents wasn't as obvious.

Still – they say that the best things come in small boxes. I'm afraid I have to accept that I'm small and getting smaller. But I do find myself wanting to correct the nurses at the hospital when they measure me before another heart test.

'I'm still 5'1½" not 5ft nothing', I want to say!!

My parents' wedding photograph 1918. Can you see the box under the carpet where my mother is standing?

34. THE FABULOUS SMELL OF FRESHLY BAKED BREAD

I love the smell of freshly baked bread. When in 1943 we moved to the flat in Wentworth Dwellings that overlooked the market, every weekday morning I woke to the gorgeous aroma of baking bread from Kossoff's bakery opposite. I now bake my own bread and rolls so I can enjoy that lovely experience regularly.

One of the advantages of having four children and four grandchildren is that I can pass on any pieces of equipment I want to upgrade, like a bread maker. My British grandson, Luke, was a willing recipient of my Panasonic bread maker, so I could in all conscience buy the latest model.

For years I had used my bread maker to make the dough and then prove and bake it in a regular long loaf tin in my normal fan oven. I always thought that the loaves that are completely finished in bread makers are too tall for us. Our appetites are not what they used to be, now Josh is 90 and I am 88, and the slices are just too big. But then Luke sent me an image of the loaf he had baked using the delay feature, so he was woken in the morning by the fantastic smell of a freshly baked loaf. I realised that I could just cut the loaf in half - eat one half and freeze the other. Works a dream!!

I still use my bread maker to make dough for rolls, which we like to have with soup. Josh and I share the cooking to fit in with our classes and it's become a tradition for me to make soup on Thursdays. I always have a variety of rolls in the freezer, including Jamie Oliver's Crumpies. If you like crumpets - the old fashioned type with big bubbles - his easy recipe is great, but our favourites are beetroot rolls. I got the original recipe for a beetroot loaf from a supermarket magazine but it works just as well for the rolls I bake in little loaf tins. You can't taste the beetroot but the colour is gorgeous.

We slice and toast these mini loaves lightly. Yummy!!

35. WW2 – THE BLITZ. EVACUATED TO DAWLISH 1940-42

I was the youngest and smallest of the 40 children evacuated to the hostel in Dawlish. The Blitz had started on September 7th 1940 and the Luftwaffe systematically bombed London for 56 of the following 57 days and nights. Many children, unhappy at being evacuated, had come back to London. Posters appeared everywhere urging parents to send their children back to the safety of the countryside.

After my awful experience evacuated to Ely, I said I wouldn't go away again, but at not quite eight years old I had no choice. I was sent off to the hostel for Jewish children in Dawlish run by *Habonim* (a Jewish youth movement). A distant cousin, who worked in a similar hostel in Teignmouth, took me there.

For the first time ever, I was petted and made much of, though I found my chores tough, especially in the depths of winter. There were several dormitories and my job was to clean the basins in each of the bedrooms before leaving for school. It wasn't too bad in the summer, but in the winter, when the water was icy and the patterns of Jack Frost covered the windows, I got chilblains on my fingers, as well as on my toes.

I had just been in trouble for refusing to comb my hair or wash on Saturdays. I had decided it was work and so forbidden on the Sabbath. The matron wrote to ask my parents whether this was their choice. They wrote back saying it was all nonsense and so I was thoroughly told off by her.

However, to my surprise, my parents agreed to pay for me to have piano lessons. Mr Lawson was the organist at the local church and also taught the piano. A short tubby man, I would sit next to him entranced as he played for me. He smoked continuously, even while he was playing, the ash dropping unheeded onto his waistcoat. I expected a pianist to have long slender hands, but his nicotine-stained fingers were short and stubby, with coarse dark hair on the backs. But he made magic with them.

He invited me to come to the local church to hear him play the organ on Sunday, but I knew my Orthodox parents would be horrified so I never did, though the love of music was with me forever. I have had many piano tutors since, but none will ever compare with my first teacher, Mr Lawson.

In Dawlish aged 8

36. MY TWOPENNY CLUB ROW FORTUNE

If I had been good and not been cheeky, on Sunday my dad would take me to Club Row to see the animals. One week I asked if I could buy a twopenny fortune. The fortune seller had a yellow budgerigar perched on his shoulder and a tray stuffed with rows of little envelopes suspended around his neck. When you handed over your two pennies, the budgie would fly down, pick out one of the envelopes with its beak and hand it to you. The bystanders watched in silence as I opened the envelope.

'You will win the football pools, get married and have four children,' I read out to a round of applause.

I managed two of the three but winning the football pools wasn't one of them!!

I had qualified in dentistry and was halfway through my medical training when we got married in 1956. By the time I completed my second post as a house physician, and was now able to work outside a hospital, I was five months pregnant with Simon.

Unfortunately, I developed raised blood pressure and fluid retention towards the end of my pregnancy and was prescribed strict rest. I was bored out of my mind. Two weeks before Simon was due, I was delighted when Josh's cousins invited us for dinner. Both of them were great cooks and *bon viveurs.*

In 1960 we weren't generally aware of the dangers of alcohol in pregnancy so when we arrived, we were greeted with a glass of dry sherry, as was the custom. I had two glasses of a very good Hungarian red wine with the delicious meal and a snifter of brandy with my after-dinner coffee.

Then my waters broke and Josh drove us to the hospital in our old Morris 8 banger as fast as it would go.

When I arrived at the hospital where I'd trained, the midwife settled me in and sent Josh back for the case I kept ready for such an emergency.

'Nothing's happening at the moment,' she said. 'Just take this *Seconal* (quinalbarbitone). It will help you to sleep. As it's your first baby it could be ages yet.'

'I really don't need it. I'm more like a dormouse than anything. I'll be asleep in no time.'

'Be good now, Dr Waterman,' she said. So I swallowed the capsule.

But soon my contractions started.

'I'll just give you something for the pain,' the midwife said.

'It's not really hurting,' I said.

'Be good,' she said, and gave me an injection of Pethidine.

By now, I'd had a glass of sherry, two large glasses of wine, a brandy, a capsule of Seconal and an injection of Pethidine. I was as high as a kite!!

I knew a few dirty songs and sang them at the top of my voice, but I knew a lot more hymns and started to sing them while the midwife exhorted me to push.

Finally, her instructions got through to me and my gorgeous baby boy was born. Amazingly, the moment I held Simon in my arms, I was stone cold sober. What incredible beings we are!!

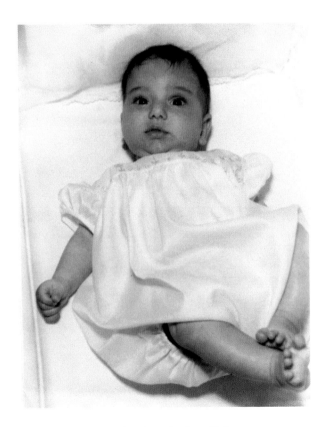

Simon in the days before Babygros.

37. A DREIDEL FOR *HANUKAH*

Until I was about eight years old, and my Aunt Jennie bought me a china doll with eyes that opened and closed, the only bought toy I had was a *dreidel*, a little four-sided wooden spinning top. It was kept in a glass-fronted cupboard with other precious things like the *Kiddush* cups and *Menorah* (8-branched candlestick) brought out year after year for *Hanukah* (the Feast of Lights; which commemorates the rededication by the Maccabees of the second temple after its desecration by the Syrians).

Each side of the dreidel bears a letter of the Hebrew alphabet: נ (*nun*), ג (*gimel*), ה (*hei*), ש (*shin*) – shorthand for the rules of a gambling game: Nun stands for the Yiddish word *nisht* ("nothing"), Hei stands for *halb* ("half"), Gimel for *gants* ("all"), and Shin for *shtel ayn* ("put in"). Nowadays they are often regarded as representing *nes gadol hayah sham* ("a great miracle happened there").

Anything else we played with was picked up from Petticoat Lane market refuse, begged or nicked. Before the dustmen cleared them all away, we rescued clean orange boxes from the fruiterer's rubbish to make a wicket and bat for the cricket we played in Wentworth Street. We'd wash a tinned fruit can for 'Tin Can Tommy', while chalk for hopscotch, and for cryptic messages about who loved whom, was nicked from school. We wheedled cigarette cards from adults as soon as we saw them lighting up, while lengths of string dropped in the street were precious finds for playing ever more intricate cat's cradle.

In our present more affluent time, it's hard to imagine what it was like for the poor who had absolutely no discretionary income. There was no spare money for frivolities like toys – unless you counted the fragile little celluloid dolls the Rag and Bone man gave you in exchange for whatever secondhand goodies you could bring him.

But if you are poor, and all your friends and neighbours are as poor or poorer, you don't know what you're missing and even a well-used *dreidel* is fun.

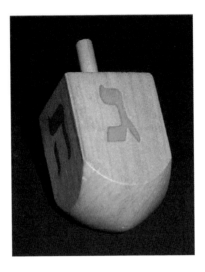

A wooden *dreidel*

38. ME AND MY TONSILS

It was still dark when my mother shook me awake and whispered, 'Get up and don't wake your sister.'

After my grandmother died, I shared the big double bed with my middle sister, Hannah. I crept to the bottom of the bed past her feet and crawled out.

When I reached for the Cornflakes my mother smacked my hand away.

'You know you mustn't eat before an operation.'

I would have liked to ask what an operation was but I could tell that my mother was already cross, especially when I couldn't find my shoes. Somehow they'd got right under the bed and I had to crawl in amongst the dust bunnies to get them.

She marched me up Wentworth Street to Commercial Street where we caught a tram to Grays Inn Road and the old Royal Free Hospital.

I was quickly admitted, and my mother left. I had my tonsils out that day and I remember waking up with an awful sore throat, helped a bit by a scoop each of vanilla and strawberry ice cream.

Once my throat eased a bit, I had a great time playing with the other children. We had Ludo and Snakes and Ladders to play with, but the very best was chasing over and under the beds – at least, until the nurses told us off.

I was almost sorry when the nurse said we would be going home. My mother was always late for everything and I was left all alone in the waiting room as the others were collected one by one. She finally came, only to tell me off because I'd spilled something down my jumper.

In those days it was just a couple of bad sore throats and out came your tonsils. Now we realise that the tonsils are large lymphatic glands that have an important role to play in our immune system.

Fortunately, there were still a few indications for tonsillectomy when I was a young Ear, Nose and Throat (ENT) house surgeon in 1959. Because I had already qualified as a dentist as well as a doctor, and I suppose seemed steady and sensible, my consultant allowed me to have my own operating list, removing tonsils and adenoids. We took out tonsils by grabbing them in a steel snare and nipping them off. Usually we removed the adenoids as well by scraping them out. I loved it all.

By that time, Josh and I were married and, though I would have loved to have trained as a surgeon, I felt that as a married woman I was unlikely to get far. In my hospital, there was only one woman consultant surgeon (unmarried, of course) and that was the usual state of affairs.

Hannah was the prettiest one of the three of us

39. HAPPY FORTHCOMING *HANUKAH* EVERYONE
As we lit the *Hanukah* candles we sang

מָעוֹז צוּר יְשׁוּעָתִי
Maoz tzur y'shuati

But instead of
לְךָ נָאֶה לְשַׁבֵּחַ
תִּכּוֹן בֵּית תְּפִלָּתִי
L'cha naeh l'shabeach
Tikon beit t'filati

under our breaths Hannah and I sang

The cat's in the cupboard
And it can't catch me

Large menorah at the Jewish Museum Camden

40. IT'S FANTASTIC HAVING A DAUGHTER

Of course, I loved my two sons. Still do, even though they're both now bald and getting on for 60, but daughters are extra special.

When I was pregnant with Louise in 1966, ultrasounds were not yet in general use so I was prepared to have a another son or a daughter. As babies, the boys had slept in carrycots until they were old enough for a proper cot but one of the craft workers, who made wicker rattles and balls for our John Dobbie toyshop, made me a gorgeous wicker cradle. I spent ages lining and trimming it with a delicate pale turquoise checked fabric – the colour would do for either sex.

My labour started in the small hours and Josh took me and the boys – then six and four – to the nursing home. I hadn't been able to book in to have another baby at the hospital where I qualified, as I was outside their catchment area and it was a normal pregnancy. The local maternity hospital was fully booked around the time I was due.

The boys were complaining that they were hungry when Josh left me tucked into a pleasant room with a lovely coal fire. He decided to take them to Covent Garden, then still a busy Fruit, Vegetable and Flower Market, and where there were cafes open all-night for the market porters.

Josh ordered sandwiches and hot milk for the boys. The counter assistant poured hot water over a couple of teaspoons.

'Better to sterilise them for the little boys,' she said.

Louise finally made her appearance in the evening after Josh had been up to see me and then taken the boys home to bed. It was love at first sight with this adorable little 6½ pound dark-haired little scrap. I'd breast fed the boys and she was as easy as they had been.

The only trouble was that I'd not eaten all day in case a problem would have arisen and I'd needed an emergency C-section. I was starving. I asked the nurse for something to eat but, being a private facility, the senior nurse had locked the fridges and food stores when she left at night. Luckily, I was so tired that I fell asleep.

It was a nice comfortable room with pleasant friendly nurses but a bit slap-dash. On the few days I stayed there, after dinner I tucked my little one under the bedclothes with just her nose out so she could breathe. To my delight the nurses forgot to take her to the nursery. When she cried I fed her and she soon went back to sleep. Bliss.

I loved dressing her in pretty clothes and now she chooses pretty things for her daughter – and for me.

We mothers of daughters are the luckiest in the world.

Louise sees the joke

41. MY DAUGHTER THE PHYSICS PROFESSOR

We've all heard the very un-PC Jewish Mother jokes, including those about her calling out to rescue her drowning children 'Save my son, the doctor' or 'Save my grandson, the psychiatrist!!' Well, my eldest son <u>is</u> a doctor, a Professor, and our youngest is a Professor of Physics.

She nearly didn't make it though. I was 34 weeks pregnant and we had just been to visit our elder son after his ear operation. A trickle of liquid down my legs indicated that my membranes had broken six weeks early. At the maternity department, just across the road, the obstetrics registrar advised me to rest.

'See if you can get this little one a bit more mature, Abby,' he said. 'Safer at home, though. Less chance of picking up a hospital infection.'

After about a week, mostly in bed, my contractions started. I was disappointed that the ambulance man wouldn't put on the bell.

'It's only for emergencies,' he said. 'Looks as if it will be some time yet.'

Josh met me at the labour ward and almost as soon as I arrived my contractions started in earnest. As my baby was premature I couldn't have a painkilling injection and had to push very carefully. Premature babies need to be delivered very gently to avoid damage to their brains.

Jane came out bright pink and crying loudly. She weighed 4½ pounds, which was a good weight for a premature baby. After letting us have a quick look at her, she was whisked off to the prem baby unit and I was deposited in a side room in the post-natal ward. I quickly fell asleep. When I awoke, I asked several times when I could see my baby, but was always told they were busy in the prem unit.

Finally, the Professor of Paediatrics came to see me.

'I would get your husband to come back, Abby,' he said. 'I'm afraid your baby's not doing well. She's developed Respiratory Disease of the Newborn. She may not make the night.'

I begged to go down and see her, but he said there was a lot going on in the prem unit.

'Better not,' he replied.

They made me take a sleeping pill and I dozed off, waking several times in the night.

Finally, night sister came in, finishing her rounds. I was almost too scared to ask how my baby was doing, was she still alive, but she said she'd go down to the prem unit and see. She was back in a few minutes that seemed like hours as I waited to hear the worst.

'She's holding her own,' she said. 'You can pop down for a few minutes.'

My little girl was in an incubator, panting away, trying to take in enough oxygen, tubes coming out of everywhere.

'You're so lucky you had her here, Dr Waterman,' the prem unit sister said. 'RDN is prof's speciality and her distress was picked up really early.'

I knew Respiratory Disease of the Newborn was a condition in which the lungs didn't expand properly at birth and at that time was often fatal.

When Josh brought our other three children in to see her, they looked like giants compared with her.

Jane pulled through, became a competent flautist, so her lungs were obviously not permanently damaged, was as bright as a button and is now an internationally known Professor of Physics.

Just shows that where there's life there's hope!!

Jane with one of the hand-embroidered balls we sold in our John Dobbie educational toyshop.

42. THE PHANTOM HEAD - OR HOW I BECAME A DENTIST

I was 17, almost 18, when I started my dental training in October 1949. In our first year, like the medical students, we studied Anatomy, Physiology and Biochemistry with, for us, the addition of Dental Anatomy – the structure and function of the teeth and jaws. The second year was spent learning to make and fit Partial and Full dentures (Prosthetics). We spent our two final years in the Conservation Department learning how to do fillings, gold inlays and bridges and how to pull teeth either in the General Anaesthetics room (always called the Gas Room because we used nitrous oxide gas as an anaesthetic) or under Local Anaesthetic injection in the Locals Room. We also carried out some minor oral surgery like removing redundant gum flaps or trimming the gum around the teeth – Gingivectomy – and learned how to Scale and Polish teeth – these were the days before this was delegated to Oral Hygienists.

We learned how to remove decay (caries), trim the cavity so a filling would hold – in those days often mercury amalgam – and also how to cast and fit gold fillings when they were more suitable.

All this was carried out using a Phantom Head – not a Virtual Head (hardly even dreamt of in 1951) – but a solid one made of metal with a jaw that opened and closed.

Teeth that weren't too broken down - perhaps had been removed for overcrowding or because they were loose – were collected in the extraction rooms and stored in antiseptic solution. Our first task when we joined the Conservation Department was to fish out a set of 28 teeth – 4 upper and 4 lower incisors, 4 upper and lower premolars and 4 upper and lower molars. We didn't bother with third molars – wisdom teeth – not everybody had them anyhow.

I developed enough skill to get a Distinction in my Dental Surgery Finals but for me it was always a question of thinking 'right a bit' and 'left a bit'. I wasn't a natural and had to plan very carefully how to go about any task, though I learned to be competent.

But during our course we had lectures on Medicine, Surgery and Pathology and I fell in love with the whodunit of Pathology – but that's also another story.

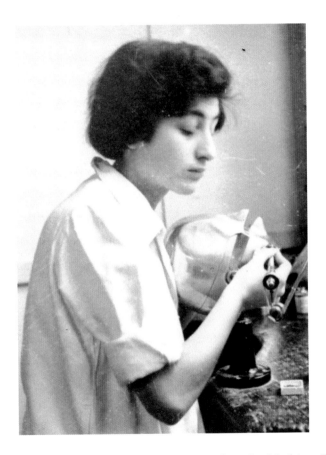

As a student in 1951, removing decay in a tooth embedded in a Phantom Head

43. HURRAH! WE MADE IT TO 2020

I was born in 1931. Had I been born 30 years earlier, would I have survived breast cancer, a fractured hip, wrist and ankle and, in 2016, a near-fatal heart attack, when my notes were labelled 'Do Not Resuscitate' if the second attempt to wean me off a ventilator failed?

I remember in 1999 thinking 'Well I'm 69, very nearly three score and ten, will I make it to the Millennium – and all the predicted computer crashes that never happened?'

And now here we are in 2020 and I'm still hanging on at age 88 thanks to the amazing advances in medicine. We take x-rays, radiotherapy and antibiotics for granted as well as the even more amazing robotics. My heart has two metal stents keeping my blocked coronary arteries open and powerful drugs are helping my heart to remodel itself. All unimaginable in my parents' youth.

I'm afraid I'm very superstitious, although 13 is my lucky number. I never walk under ladders and there was no way I would even think about what I was going to post about the New Year before the very last stroke of midnight – just in case I didn't make it!!

Lovely watching the fireworks on the London Eye with our daughter and son-in-law. Shame this year, the grandchildren couldn't make it.

Fireworks on the London Eye from our balcony

44. ON BEING A GOURMET COOK – OR NOT

When Josh and I got married in 1956, I had two dishes in my repertoire – a simple omelette and minestrone soup. My mother was a plain cook, with a limited range of dishes – cold fried fish on Friday night, *cholent* (chicken and potatoes left on a low gas all night) on Saturday and braised or roast beef or boiled chicken on other days. Our main meal was at lunchtime – our dinner — always a rushed meal, because my father and older sisters had only half an hour for lunch and I had to get back to school. For supper we had egg on toast or sardines on toast so I could add those to my range of expertise and of course from my student days baked beans on toast. Josh on the other hand came from a family of good cooks – his paternal grandfather had been a baker in Poland – and so Josh was a much better cook than I.

I gradually extended my range with the help of recipes in newspapers and magazines but then, when I finished my second post as a house physician and was five months pregnant with Simon, I decided to take a 6 week full time Good Housekeeping Cookery Course held in basement kitchens in Mayfair. It was an excellent course ranging from the simplest dishes – how to boil an egg or mash a potato – to Black Forest Gateaux and various loaves of bread.

When you have four children, and two of them are ravenous boys, you go more for quantity than variety. I got used to serving a three course meal and then having the boys ask for a 'sarnie' – or two. They were still 'starving'.

After I retired in 1991, I took a wide range of courses at Further Education Colleges including cooking. The best was Joyce's course (sadly she's no longer with us) at Morley College. It was a 'Cook and Eat' course. You paid a modest sum for the ingredients that Joyce lugged in each week, and then you paired off to cook a three course meal. I think I took the course three times – Joyce had a huge variety of tried and tested recipes.

I only remember one absolute disaster.

We had one student who was always ahead of herself. Her task was to whip the cream for our Blackberry and Apple crumble and she'd got the cream prepared long before we were ready to sit down for our meal. I had to rush off for my Spanish lesson at the Mary Ward Centre in Queens Square and so was the first to be served with my desert.

I took a spoonful and spat it out. I was sure I had been poisoned. The salt and sugar – both white granules – were kept in glass jars and she hadn't bothered to check the labels. She'd used salt instead of sugar and in that concentration the salted cream tasted vile. Probably a very primitive response to ingredients that – certainly in that quantity – are bad tor us.

My favourite Fruit Cake recipe came with our first Magimix.. Keeps and freezes well.

45. FROM SHMEAR TO ETERNITY – MY LOVELY YIDDISCHE DICTIONARY

I saw Fred Kogos's dictionary online some time ago but none of the UK online booksellers I tried had a new copy at the list price of £10.99. Not only a new copy but secondhand copies were all at silly prices starting at £54. Finally, I found some secondhand copies from three USA bookstores but none of them would ship to the UK. Then, just before Christmas, a secondhand copy was listed on Amazon US. Not cheap at £23.54 including nearly £4 postage, but so well worth it. It's in very good condition, the paper slightly foxed but no underlines or highlighting.

It is all in Roman script not Hebrew – much easier for me. Yiddish->
English then English -> Yiddish and then pages of Yiddish proverbs.

It made me quite weepy, reading the proverbs my late mother used to
encourage or berate me with. Never thought a dictionary would make tears
come to my eyes.

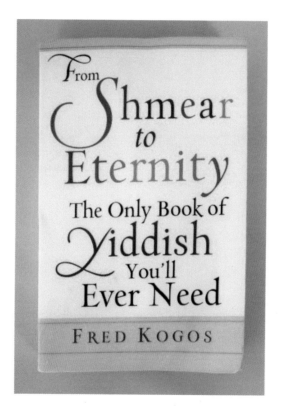

My new secondhand *Yiddische* dictionary

46. OUR FIRST JOHN DOBBIE TOYSHOP

It was 1962. Simon was 2½ and Bernard was 4 months old. Josh was working full time in our dental practice up in town and I was working part time in the dental practice I had set up in our small terrace house in Wimbledon.

Despite the fact that we were both working, we were overdrawn, having taken on too big a mortgage. We cast about for ways of making some extra money and finally decided to open an educational toyshop. It was such an ordeal getting two small boys ready to go up to town to find some toys that didn't fall to pieces almost straightaway. The word you thought of then, when someone said 'toys', was 'broken'!! There was an excellent toyshop owned by Paul and Marjorie Abbatt in Wimpole Street and Heal's had some good toys, particularly at Christmas, but it wasn't easy dragging the boys up to town.

We approached local agents in Wimbledon village only to be told none of the shops ever changed hands. All of them had been there for ages. Then, just before Christmas, one of the agents rang to say a small shop had come on the market.

It was ideal. A reasonable rent for a small bow-fronted shop – just one's image of *Ye Olde Toy Shoppe*.

Winter 1962-3 was the coldest for years and we almost said 'no'. I remember inspecting the premises, still with a post-pregnancy weak bladder, and finding the loo frozen solid.

Having managed to borrow £500 between the bank and a friend of my sister's, we spent £250 on fitting it out and £250 on stock. If we visited any shop that stocked attractive sturdy toys, we turned them over to look at the labels to find the suppliers. We also managed to find some craftworkers making beautiful toys to order, as well as sturdy wooden toys imported from Scandinavia.

I wrote to all the Sunday glossies to tell them our shop would be opening at Easter and to our great good fortune the Woman's Page editor, the wonderful late Moira Keenan, wrote about us on the Sunday before Easter. Fantastic!!

That Wimbledon shop later moved to a larger shop in the High Street and we opened a second shop in Putney. We never made much money out of them though it was a wonderful experience. Finally, having had enough of running John Dobbie, we sold the Putney shop in a property deal, and the Wimbledon shop to a couple who had opened a shop like ours elsewhere.

I decided to return to medicine, hoping to specialise in dental pathology. The professor who'd invited me to come and see him, if and when I was ready, had retired and when I approached his replacement for a job, he turned me down saying 'A married woman with four children and no expertise – you've nothing to offer.'

Five years later I was a consultant pathologist with an international reputation. When we met later he swore he'd never said anything of the kind – but he had!!

Simon aged 3 and me looking in at our first bow-fronted toyshop.

47. IT TAKES A NERVE TO CATCH YOURSELF A HUSBAND

As soon as I turned seventeen, the pressure was on. This was long before Computers or Internet Dating, and my mother started to worry that she'd have to find a *Shadchen* (a matchmaker) if, like a nice Jewish girl, I was to get married and have a big family. But despite my mother's fears, all I needed was the nerve.

In my early teens, eager to meet handsome young men, I got myself booked into Guy's Hospital Dental School to have my teeth seen to. I never actually got off with any of them, and I certainly never knew why I had the professor and a crowd of students around me when a new junior student took over my treatment.

I was now a senior dental student myself and treating my favourite patient. He was an elderly man who had a fund of brilliant stories of *Times Gone By*. He kept me in gales of laughter – in between me trying to get on with filling the many cavities in his teeth.

I'd had odd twinges of toothache in a lower premolar, but when I consulted our very misogynistic professor, he said he could find no cause for my pain and that I was just another hysterical young woman student.

But now I had a throbbing pain in my tooth that seemed to be bursting out of my head. I'd never experienced anything like it. If you've ever had really bad toothache you will know what I mean. It was almost unbearable.

I apologised to my patient and said I'd have to put in a temporary filling. I just couldn't go on.

He tried hard, but he couldn't help grinning.

'Don't worry, my dear,' he said. 'You get yourself seen to. Good to have an excuse to come and see you again.'

The pain had subsided a little and I was able to bid him goodbye.

I didn't know the on duty house surgeon very well, but I knew he had the reputation of being very skilful but with a sharp tongue. I expected him to be as scathing as my professor.

By now the pain had simmered down a bit. I went up to him and asked him to look at my tooth, explaining that the prof had been unable to find the source of my fleeting pain.

In very little time, he established that a right lower premolar, which had a small filling in it, was the source of my raging toothache. The very junior student at Guy's Hospital, who'd treated me all those years ago, had drilled too deep and exposed the nerve in the centre of the tooth – hence the crowd around me, watching the exposed nerve being capped off. It had lain dormant for years and was now finally giving trouble.

The house surgeon gave me an injection, removed the inflamed nerve and arranged to complete the root filling when it had settled down.

Having made a further appointment, he asked me if I'd like to come to the cinema that weekend to see *Les Enfants du Paradis*.

The rest is history. Now, four children and four grandchildren later, Josh and I have been married the best part of 64 years.

Josh as a very handsome young dental student (not me – another student in his dental chair)

48. ALL 6s AND 7s – ACCORDING TO WILL SHAKESPEARE

On my way home from seeing the audiologist about my hearing aids, I thought about all the 'falsies' now available to us. I don't have those we usually associate with the term – when I had surgery for breast cancer immediate reconstruction wasn't on offer, but I have been fitted with some of the other prosthetic replacements hardly dreamt of when Jacques in

Shakespeare's 'As You Like It' spoke of the Seven Ages of Man – from a prosthetic hip to stents in my coronary arteries and hearing aids.

In the UK by 2018 the expectation of life for men was 79.6 and for women 83.2. In Shakespeare's time, in the 16th century, the expectation of life for both was just under 40, given the high mortality during infancy and childbirth. At 40, I'd have thought myself in the prime of life and was just about to start my specialist training as a consultant pathologist. My final career was just about to begin.

'The sixth age shifts
Into the lean and slippered pantaloon,
With spectacles on nose'

'Last scene of all,
That ends this strange eventful history,
Is second childishness and mere oblivion,
Sans teeth, sans eyes, sans taste, sans everything.'

I used to be lean and wish I were again. I've more 'the fair round belly' of the Justice and I only wear slippers at home – haven't yet descended into going out in them, nor in curlers. I've most of my own teeth with only one false tooth – a bridge supported by a tooth on either side, and since having my cataracts removed and false lenses inserted, I no longer wear spectacles,. Also, I have a false hip after fracturing the neck of my right femur in Spain in 2000.

I'm not sure about the 'second childishness', though every now again, when I try to remember a word or a name, I experience the 'mere oblivion'. But so at times do my children and grandchildren. Immediately after my heart attack I virtually lost my sense of taste and some manual dexterity, but they're mostly back now.

Lucky we don't live in Shakespeare's time, when 'sans teeth, sans eyes, sans taste, sans everything' meant literally that!!

Age 6 from Rachel Mulligan's sequence '*Seven Ages of Man*' stained glass roundels illustrating the life of her father Jim Mulligan, Stained Glass Museum, Ely Cathedral

49. THE TURKEY BONE LADY

My first post after qualifying as a doctor was as a house surgeon in the Ear, Nose and Throat department. During the week I was on 24/7 but, as there were two ENT housemen, we had alternate weekends off.

It was the day after Boxing Day 1958 and we were all feeling rather fragile after the party the night before. My bleep went. It was Sister in Casualty.

'I think you're on call for ENT, Dr Waterman. Could you come down? We have a patient for you.'

I walked through the tunnel to Casualty and was greeted by Sister wearing a red paper hat.

'It's the large lady over there,' she said.

I looked across. She was enormous. She dwarfed her tiny husband.

I grinned and pointed to Sister's hat.

'My God,' she said, pulling it off. 'I've been wearing this all morning. Haven't been to bed yet. I'm off in an hour.'

'It's something I've swallowed,' my patient said. 'It's because of my daughter-in -law, Doris. She's a bit sloppy with her cooking.'

Her husband patted her fat little hand.

'She tries her best, love.'

'It was the turkey stew. My new teeth still hurt when I chew and as it was just stew I took them out to eat. Next thing there was something sticking in my throat. I tried gargling and eating dry bread but it's still there this morning.'

'Do you think you could walk over with me to the ENT department. I think you're going to need an anaesthetic for us to see what it is. It's good you haven't eaten anything this morning.'

My registrar was sitting in the surgeon's lounge looking pitiful.

'Speak very quietly,' he said. 'I think my head is going to explode. I thought we'd have a quiet day. Can you book a theatre and bleep the anaesthetist on call? I hope he's not feeling as bad as I am.'

The registrar got the turkey vertebra out easily and I took it round to recovery to show my patient.

I was off the next weekend and went shopping in the local market. I heard a voice calling 'Miss, Miss. Doctor.'

It was the turkey bone lady. I thought I had recognised her when I first saw her in Casualty but I hadn't been sure. She had quite the best fruit and vegetable stall in the market. I chose some apples and a bunch of bananas and held out a £1 note.

'That's all right, love. I owe you. You were so kind to me.'

I tried to insist but she wasn't having any. It wasn't very much, so I said thank you and backed off fast when she looked as if she was going to kiss me.

The trouble was she tried not to charge me the next time I went shopping. I couldn't have that, so I had to shop at one of the other stalls.

One day she stopped me.

'I've seen you going to her opposite. Nothing like the quality on our barrow. OK. I'll charge you then but I'll see you right. You'll have the best stuff you've ever seen.'

It wasn't fair really. All I'd done was book her in. My registrar was nursing a sore head and he was so grumpy he upset her.

It shows we all want a bit of Tender Loving Care.

A Fruit and Vegetable stall in San Sebastian

50. ON BEING A KIND SCHOOL DENTIST

I know a lot of people have awful memories of the school dentist and the gas mask they used, but I like to think I was one of the kind ones and treated the children as if they were patients in a private practice.

I'd had an LCC (London County Council) grant to cover my dental degree so I couldn't have a second grant to cover the Medical training I started in the autumn of 1953. I applied for and was awarded a Hilda Martindale Scholarship which covered my medical school fees and a small amount towards my living expenses. I was still living at home so my expenses weren't great, but medical textbooks were very expensive and I needed money to cover clothes. I approached the LCC Dental Service for a part-time job two evenings a week and was sent to a clinic in the city.

Both the nurse and I were expecting a miserable old bag, like the school dental dentists and nurses we'd met ourselves as children, so both of us were surprised and delighted. Maureen was a rosy-cheeked Somerset lass with a broad sense of humour and we hit it off at once. We spent the time between patients giggling and exchanging notes on the talent available to us and the latest fashions.

As it was an evening clinic, most of our patients were in senior school. Once they'd got over their amazement at being greeted by two young women in their 20's and reassured that I would use a local anaesthetic for any painful fillings and never use gas, they were excellent and very grateful patients. Many of those who'd been through the school dental system hated the gas mask and it left them with a permanent fear of dentists. Although at the time, it was still legal for a dentist to administer a general anaesthetic (usually nitrous oxide) on their own, I would never do so. I could carry out fillings and extractions perfectly well under local.

In our first two years at medical school, covering Anatomy, Physiology and Biochemistry, we had long holidays so I took a two-week locum appointment at a school clinic in West Ham that Christmas. The kids were fine and I again had a very pleasant nurse, but I was appalled at the poverty around me. I was brought up in the East End and we were poor but, as my mother had been a dressmaker and scoured the markets stalls for fabric remnants, I was always reasonably well dressed. Some of these children were almost in rags. I tried to persuade a young teenage boy to take off his blazer – no overcoat. I was worried about getting blood or saliva on it. When he finally agreed, I saw that on this on a freezing December day he wore only a singlet underneath.

'I only have one shirt, you see. Mum washes it every Friday night ready for school on Monday. I never wear it in the holidays.'

I carried on with my evening clinics after Josh and I got married in 1956, until we started out own dental practice where I worked on Wednesday afternoons – when the male medical students played rugger – and Saturday mornings.

And our lovely Maureen left the LCC service and came to work in our practice until she got married in turn and her husband took a job in the country.

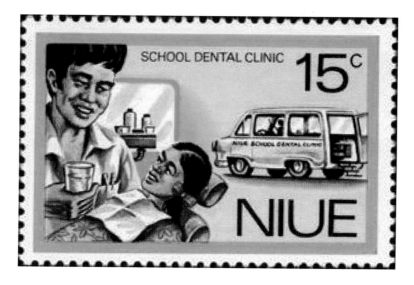

I love this 1977 New Zealand Stamp with both Dentist and Patient smiling

51. SONS AND DAUGHTERS
We have two of each but for a time all four lived abroad – our elder son in Africa, the younger in Finland, our elder daughter in the Basque Country in Spain and the baby in Switzerland. Now the boys live in the UK, though the elder often goes abroad for conferences, but the girls work permanently abroad. I hated it then and hate it now, though they come and stay with us during the year.

The girls are not often in the UK together. We have only one spare room so if they bring their partners we have to put up one pair in a hotel, like when they came over for Josh's 90th birthday.

But they are coming together this week – our elder daughter with her partner for a concert and the younger for a conference. The girls will share the spare room and Mark will have to sleep on the sofa.

They are great friends now but they weren't always. It was fine when they were little. When Jane cried for a feed Louise would pull at me – 'Ninny crying', she'd wail. 'Ninny crying.' It didn't last. When they were teenagers they were barely on speaking terms. There was only 17 months between them – Jane had been 6 weeks premature – and they seemed to have nothing in common. If we planned a trip or a holiday it was 'If she's going, I'm not.'

It got better when they both went off to Uni and now they're best friends, though they don't often meet except for events like Josh's 90th birthday last year and my heart attack in 2016.

But I do miss them. I love my sons dearly, but mothers get a completely different kind of sympathy and support from our daughters. Lucky us!!

School photo of Jane and Louise

52. *PICASSO ON PAPER* AT THE ROYAL ACADEMY

I remember when, after WW2 ended, we first saw Picasso's Cubist portraits with noses and eyes going every which way.

'My two-year old could do better than that,' was a common response at the time.

We hadn't realised that his was an intentional interpretation of reality and not lack of ability.

I retired at 60, but Josh went on working until he was 65, so I took some short trips on my own to visit Louise and her family in San Sebastian. On one of them, she and Mark took me to the rebuilt town of Guernica, where there was an exhibition about Picasso's painting *Guernica*, in memory of the bombing by Nazi warplanes at the beginning of the Spanish civil war. Not until after the death of the fascist dictator, Franco, did Picasso allow his original painting to come back to Spain. It is now housed permanently in the *Museo Reina Sofía* in Madrid.

There was a large reproduction of *Guernica,* and on either side copies of Picasso's working drawings. That's when I realised what an incredible draftsman he was. There were drawings of feet and heads - and of course his beloved bulls - all drawn in exquisite detail, before being converted into the distorted figures of his final work.

The present exhibition of Picasso's work at the Royal Academy '*Picasso on Paper*' is huge. There are works from all of his various periods. As well as his works on and with paper, there are a few oil paintings, sculptures and three dimensional collages. A veritable feast that needs more than one visit.

It was with great relief that we discovered the little bistro-type café set up at the back of the Royal Academy shop, complete with paper tablecloths and coloured pencils so you could imitate Picasso's habit of drawing on anything and everything. And good strong coffee and crispy croissants. It's a must if you can visit London.

'Les Femmes d'Alger' after Delacroix (Oil on canvas 1955)

53. LATE FOR THE WEDDING

My family was late for everything. That wasn't surprising, since my mother always started out at the time we were meant to be there – for holyday services, for the cinema, for everything. I got used to pushing past unfriendly knees and apologising 'Sorry. Sorry. So sorry'.

My parents had always gone to the Great Synagogue in Duke's Place, but the magnificent old building was bombed in 1942 and services were held in an unadorned single story temporary building. My brother-in-law, who was a *ganser macher* (big noise) in the West Ham synagogue, persuaded me to get married there and leave from their house, which was nearby.

The car to take us to the *shul* had arrived and my middle sister, Hannah, made last minute adjustments to my headdress. My elder sister, Rebecca, had recently adopted a sweet little baby girl and of course Susie needed changing urgently, just as we were about to leave. It took Rebecca ages as she fumbled with an unfamiliar terry towelling nappy and the huge safety pin. Finally, we were ready, but now we were 15 minutes late. To cap it all, there'd been a minor road accident around the corner which made us later still.

As I climbed up under the *chuppah* (wedding canopy) it was to see Josh looking absolutely ashen in his Moss Bros tuxedo and top hat. He'd been sure I'd stood him up!!

He and his parents were the opposite of mine and always on time. Once safely married, I caught being punctual from Joshua and now I'm always on time and often early. So - lots of unwanted cups of indifferent coffee while I wait for my friends to arrive or the class or meeting to start.

I was a lot slimmer then!!

54. MY GORGEOUS BASQUE GRAND-DAUGHTER

Until this last year, our elder daughter, Louise, our son-in-law, Mark, and our two Basque grandchildren spent New Year's Eve with us, either here in London or in the small house in the South of Spain we owned for a time after I retired. As soon as our grandchildren were old enough not to choke on them, they joined us eating a grape on each toll of Big Ben in the UK, or on the peal of the *Puerta del Sol* bell in Madrid – a Basque custom.

But this year our grand-daughter Susan, who is now a qualified physio-therapist, had other commitments, as did her younger brother, Adrian, who is at Uni. We missed them. It just wasn't the same without them.

To our surprise, and delight, Susan popped over last week for a few days' R & R (rest and recreation). The practice where she works was closed while some building works were carried out.

Having children is fabulous but having grandchildren is even better. Perhaps because discipline isn't a grandparent's responsibility and you can spoil them rotten.

Two year old Susan saying 'Hullo' to the little toddler in the mirror

55. TWO FOOTBALLERS IN THE FAMILY

Neither Josh nor I are much good at sports. I was put into the Star Gym Class at school but that was more for effort than for ability. I couldn't keep up with all the vaulting and jumping and had to give up after a few weeks.

However, Josh and I used to play squash a couple of times a week when we were first married and lived just up the road from the medical school where I was a student. All that ended when I became pregnant and we moved to Wimbledon. The damp furnished basement flat, where we lived when we first got married, was convenient both for my lectures and our dental practice, but not suitable for a baby. Since then, we've both tried exercise classes from time to time but we've not persisted. They are just not us.

Our Basque grandchildren, Susan and Adrian, on the other hand, are keen sportsmen. Both played football for their local *Añorga* youth team when they were at school. Adrian, who is at Uni, coaches that team a couple of evenings a week and Susan, who is now a qualified physiotherapist and works at a local clinic during the week, is physio-therapist at weekends both to the age 14 boys' *Real Sociedad* football team and the girls 16-18 team.

Mark, their father, is retired and does Pilates with our daughter, Louise. She recently ran the local 5 km race for Women's Day. Both are keen walkers.

Luckily, Susan and Adrian managed to inherit sporty genes not our couch potato traits. Now I have got to 88 and Josh to 90 we think it's probably a bit late to change.

Susan in her football gear

56. SHUT AWAY FOR FOUR MONTHS??

It's not compulsory yet, but for us elderly folk it's almost certainly coming. By chance, I passed our local library at the weekend so I collected some more books – now 13 in all. They're a mixture – mainly my favourite whodunits, but also some poetry and a collection of Oscar Wilde's witty remarks. I've still got half a dozen of my own books to read – some I bought and some left by Louise when she paid us a flying visit last month.

Daily exercise should help. When our granddaughter popped over from San Sebastian I was jealous of her fancy sports watch. Too mean to buy an expensive one like hers, I ordered a much less pricy *Letscom* fitness tracker. My hip replacement has been painful for years and I gave up on exercise classes for the over 50s, so I started by doing 10 minutes of mixed exercises each day. Yesterday I was able to do that much twice. Luckily our flat has a long corridor so I start by walking up and down 10 or more times.

I'll try to complete the sequel to my memoir *Woman in a White Coat* which I finished in 2017 as I was recovering from the heart attack that nearly took me off. I'm aiming to get back to writing every day. It's easy to get lazy, but if I'm going to be a virtual prisoner for 4 months I'll need to structure my time.

And I've even started sorting and clearing out the kitchen drawers. Amazing how much stuff we have accumulated that we're never going to use again!!

A mixture of various genres. As you see from the bookmarks, I always have at least two books on the go

57. SELF-ISOLATED AND BORED??

If you too are bored, may I suggest you read my memoir *Woman in a White Coat*? A young Jewish girl grows up in Petticoat Lane in the 1930s. Born when the Great Depression was at its height, in spite of being poor, she grows up to become a dentist, a doctor, an entrepreneur, a consultant pathologist and cancer researcher, as well as a wife and mother of four. The highs and lows of an 88-year long life.

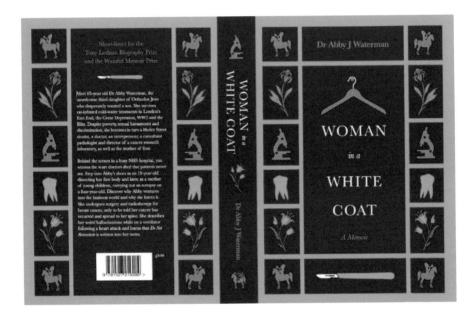

58. MORE BOOKS WAITING TO BE READ IN OUR 4 MONTHS IN ISOLATION

The books I borrowed from the library are mainly fun books, light and maybe a little silly. The books that sit on the little desk in our bedroom are books we bought or were given as birthday presents. You can see which are Josh's. He's the one who likes biographies. The only biography that is mine is my memoir. It's there so I can refer to it while writing the sequel and check I'm not repeating myself.

As you see from the titles of the books, I've developed an interest in the brain. When I was training as a pathologist, I worked for a month at the Hospital for Neurological Disorders. For me, the brain was an organ I removed at post-mortem, fixed in formalin for six months and then examined thin slices under the microscope.

In the early 1970s, MRIs were just an experimental procedure. We didn't dream that we would ever be able to look at patient's brains in an fMRI and see which part of the brain was functional and lit up. At that time, our knowledge was mainly based on what happened when parts of the brain were removed by surgery or by accident - which functions were lost when that part was damaged or lost.

Maybe when I grow up I'll have one more career as a neurophysiologist – if I survive the latest plague!!

The books on our desk waiting to be read.

59. 4 MONTHS IN DUALITUDE

As we are 88 and 90, we'll be confined for at least 4 months in our 9th floor flat. Luckily, we have a balcony that gets the sun in the afternoon. With the weather turning fine, we'll be able to sit outside and read while getting a South of France tan. Luckily, we went to the library just before this plague blew up and I still have six books left to read. My lovely Aunt Jenny gave me her complete set of Dickens – the Hazell, Watson and Viney Ltd edition with illustrations by Phiz. If push comes to shove, I'll re-read all 16 volumes. I was recovering from one of my several broken bones when I last ploughed my way through them all.

I planned on using this time to get on with the sequel to *Woman in a White Coat*, learn another Bach Two Part Invention for the piano, and keep up with my Ancient Greek, but like my New Year resolutions, they fell at the first hurdle!!

We have a very pleasant newish Waitrose nearby in Nine Elms and the last two occasions we went before being confined to our home we had been sent a page of £4-off vouchers to use if we spent £40. We have always done most of our big grocery shopping in the Tesco and Sainsburys in Cromwell Road, only topping up with a few odds and ends in the more expensive Waitrose. On the first occasion, we made up the £40 with toilet paper and on the second with bread flour and yeast – I bake all our bread. Must have earned some good points with a Higher Power to make just those choices.

So, instead of being virtuous, and writing and practising and learning, I've been baking and cooking double quantities of dishes – eating half and freezing the other half. It's so satisfying, starting off with some uninteresting looking powders, making the most heavenly smell, and then producing a great looking crusty loaf of bread.

The manager of our flats has set up a *Whatsapp* group so there are offers of help and friendship. And we all come to our balconies and windows to clap for the NHS on Thursdays at 8pm.

I hope those of you reading my memoir will take some comfort from the stories of hard times past we all came through.

My precious set of Dickens from Aunt Jenny.

60. STICKY BUNS

I've no idea who taught me this, but it was my party piece as a young child, recited with a suitable lisp!!

Johnny bought a penny bun
In the baker's shop
It was such a pretty bun
Sticky at the top

Came a hungry doggy by
Says Johnny 'Ave a bit'
The doggy liked it very much
And soon the bun was gone

Came a fine fat gentleman
Watching all the fun
'Here y'are Johnny. Here's a penny
Buy another bun.'

These buns are modified from Mary Berry's Hot Cross Buns Recipe – now Hot Nought Buns. On my daughter Louise's advice, I made the dough in the breadmaker and proved and baked the buns in the oven. I'm thinking of using the same recipe to make a fruit loaf – when there's a bit more room in the freezer.

That's the trouble with time on your hands – it's more fun to cook and freeze something than write up more memories or catch up on my Ancient Greek.

12 delicious Hot Nought Buns

61. RYE BREAD AND BEIGELS/ BAGELS (TOMATOES/ TOMATOES)

Living in Petticoat Lane opposite the Kossoff and Grodzinski bakeries, a slice or two of rye bread and butter accompanied every meal – without butter if it was a meat meal. My grandmother, who lived with us until she died in 1937, had long since given up her pitch on the corner of Wentworth Street. She sold beigels there until my parents got married in 1918 and she moved with them to Old Kent Road.

It's always lovely having my daughter Louise and her Basque husband Mark come to stay and one of their special treats is to buy us a couple of sliced rye loaves and some beigels from the *Beigel Bake* shop at the end of Brick Lane. My hip is still too sore for me to walk far, and parking is difficult around Brick Lane, so we've given up going ourselves.

They were due to come for Easter, but who knows when air traffic will resume? They are hoping to visit us in August, even if it means seeing us from 2 metres away!!

So, it's down to making my own rye and caraway loaf and beigels. The loaf I make in the breadmaker tastes fine and authentic, but it isn't an oval glazed loaf like the traditional one. I haven't made any beigels for some time – it's a bit of a faff having to boil as well as prove the dough – but just writing about them makes me long for some. Maybe tomorrow.

A traditional tasting rye and caraway loaf but not the traditional shape

62. DELICIOUS HOME MADE BEIGELS/ BAGELS

Having written about my grandmother selling beigels on the corner of Wentworth Street and Goulston Street, I just had to have some. As an 88 year old self-isolating, I can't go and buy them from *Beigel Bake* in Brick Lane, so I got out the *Lekue* Silicone Beigel moulds I bought ages ago. They are brown perforated moulds rather like Witch's Hats with a very narrow point you push the balls of dough over to give a neat central hole. You prove them and then boil them on the moulds.

Our English granddaughter, Becca, not to be outdone, rolled her dough into sausages, curled them into a ring, moistened the ends and stuck the ends together. I just glazed mine with milk and left it at that, but Becca who, like her brother Luke, is Vegan, glazed hers with Oat Milk and decorated some with poppy seeds and some with sesame seeds. They look fabulous on her *Whatsapp* message.

She and her partner got the coronavirus early on, fortunately quite mildly, so Becca has been able to go back to working for the charity that distributes unwanted food from supermarkets and restaurants to the needy.

I would love to be able to see the family again in the flesh. Zoom is great but there's nothing like a hug from the family.

Can't say my bagels taste exactly like the professional ones but they're pretty good– and they freeze well. It's an important consideration when you are just two old people desperately trying not to put on too much weight!!

Not as perfect as those from *Beigel Bake* but they taste fine

63. GOING WALKIES

Being very much older than 70 and having an impressive medical history, I am designated as vulnerable and have to be confined for 16 weeks. I can set my inexpensive *Lescom* Sports Watch not only to time my exercise but to calculate the distance I travel and the calories I use. It certainly makes me realise how much exercise I need to do to work off one of my favourite chocolate digestive biscuits or a few peanuts!!

Our flat is arranged around a corridor – about 15 of my short steps – and I try to do at least 10 minutes of exercise a day, including pacing up and down it and touching my toes umpteen times. I do a mixture of exercises from the NHS website, some from the class that ran at my GP surgery and some given me by the various physiotherapists who tried to deal with my painful hip that followed a fracture and hip replacement. The NHS recommends at least 150 minutes exercise a week but I don't manage two sessions every day, but apparently even 10 minutes of exercise a day is better than nothing.

Josh and I go for a walk every weekend along the Thames Embankment, often resting on a bench outside Tate Britain. We leave the steps clear for exercisers – cheering them on and exhorting them to go up and down 100 times. So far no-one has done more than ten times. This Sunday an old Chinese grandfather guided a pretty little toddler up and down and round the corner.

We live on the 9th floor with a balcony, so the lovely weather we've had recently has allowed me to get a bit of a tan. Unfortunately, I've finished all 13 of my library books so I'm now reading on my Kindle – books from Kindle itself and some from our free local Cloud Library.

When I bought my Kindle Fire I also got a matte screen to apply so I can read in bright sunshine. It's a great device, but I think I'll always prefer real paper books.

TATE BRITAIN IS CLOSED
A view of the steps, so useful for exercise, and the bench where we rest in the sun after our walk.

64. IS A SQUARE *CHALLAH* OK??

Well it's actually not square – it's rectangular. I have in my time made a conventional *challah* plaited and tapering to both ends, as well as a round *challah*, but now there are only the two of us we prefer our bread to be loaf shaped.

It started when we first got married in 1956. I was a medical student, working a couple of evenings a week as a school dentist, and Josh was working as an assistant in a dental practice in North London. After a quick breakfast, we would each hurry off, not meeting until the evening. It wasn't until dinner that we had time to sit down together. I had lunch with my fellow medical students in the medical school refectory while Josh would make do with a couple of sandwiches. Even when I had qualified as a doctor, had 4 children, and with Josh had set up an educational toyshop and then become a consultant pathologist, dinner time was our time together. To begin with, I had lunch in the consultants' dining room but the food was so good and the desserts so delicious that I started to put on too much weight. Finally, I gave up lunch altogether.

Even when we both retired, dinner was our main meal and Josh went on having a sandwich for lunch. A rectangular loaf is most convenient for that, and surely a plaited loaf is still a *Challah* – even if the shape is unconventional. You just have to say or think the word *Challah* and you can imagine the delicious smell.

BTW – I love Poppy Seed cake but I don't like poppy seeds on *Challah* or on beigels!!

My delicious 'square' *Challah*.

65. THE IMPERIAL WAR MUSEUM – A.K.A BEDLAM

This week we changed our walk from the Victoria Embankment to the grounds around the Imperial War Museum in Lambeth Road. It was a lovely spring day and the roses edging the lawn outside were in full bloom.

The actual building was constructed as the Bethlem Asylum for the Insane in St George's Fields, moving there from Bridewell and then Moorfields in 1828.

Probably from as early as 1598, visitors were allowed to come and laugh and poke at the poor inmates. Known as 'Bedlam', it was a popular stop on the London tourist trail and a source of income for the hospital and staff. When the asylum moved to Beckenham in 1936, the Imperial War Museum transferred to Lambeth from the Imperial Institute in South Kensington..

I first saw the Imperial War Museum from my room in the clinic opposite, on a snowy evening in February 1990. Though still attached to various tubes after surgery for breast cancer, I was able to walk around and look out of the window. The snow was no longer falling, but it lay thick on the windowsill, glistening under the starlit sky. The elegant snow-covered Imperial War Museum across the road, with its tall cupola, looked like a fairy castle in the moonlight.

I needed cheering up. As a consultant pathologist, who had worked in a cancer hospital for 4 years, I had carried out numerous autopsies on women with breast cancer. Virtually all the women I encountered with breast cancer had died of the disease. When I lectured on the subject, I pointed out how good the prognosis for breast cancer was, but I still thought it would prove fatal for me. It didn't – and that was 30 years ago. Now the outlook for patients with breast cancer is better than ever.

I can't decide whether it is better or worse to be in the 'trade' if you are a doctor and have a life-threatening disease. Of course, the surgeon, the anaesthetist and the radiotherapist were all friends as well as colleagues. I could stop the breast surgeon in the corridor and ask for a quick word about the hard lump I found while having a shower. But it also meant that I was well aware of the worst possible outcomes and because I was a doctor I felt I had to be extra brave, not make a fuss or 'come it'.

Although I had long since retired, when I was admitted with a near-fatal heart attack in 2016, I was treated more like a colleague than a non-medical patient, who might not understand the medical terms and find being in a hospital frightening. For me, a hospital is almost home from home and the antiseptic smell is reassuring rather than threatening.

In normal times the two huge 15 inch naval guns in front of the portico would have been swarming with children.

66. BIG PACKS AT THE SUPERMARKETS

Yes, we are fortunate – being elderly and vulnerable we can get slots at supermarkets but we do miss being able to choose our own fruit and vegetables. The two of us can cope with a 2.5kg bag of potatoes if we keep the potatoes cool and in the dark but 1kg of carrots is just too much.

OK – so I've made carrot and orange soup, had sliced carrots as a vegetable and spiralized some with the remains of a courgette to make a pretty combination of carrot and courgette spaghetti as a vegetable but there was still 1/3 of a bag left. You can order some single fruits and veggies but you can't choose the size. I ordered a leek and the one I was sent was a foot long and nearly 1½" in diameter. Almost half was composed of dark green earthy tough leaves. I would never have chosen it, had I been able to go to the supermarket in person.

My English granddaughter is a great Vegan cook and sends me images of her very professional looking bread. Not to be outclassed, I got down the *Bread* book by Christine Ingram and Jennie Shapter to look for something new. To my delight I found their Carrot and Fennel Seed bread. Absolutely delicious.

I reduced the amount of fennel seeds to 1 teaspoon but I think when I make it again I'll omit the seeds. My Carrot Bread will now join my Beetroot Bread and Square *Challah* fun loaves.

Love the orange carrot flecks

67. OLD DOGS AND NEW TRICKS

Yes, we can learn new tricks!! I didn't think that at age 88 Social Media were my thing but I've written nearly 70 posts on Facebook since last August and I regularly Zoom with the children and my Writing Circle.

Last week I started an online course at CityLit - 'Extended History of Modern Art in 50 Works' with an excellent young women tutor, Sarah Jaffray. There are 16 of us in the class – 12 women and 4 men. This is an unusual mix. Most Further Education classes I've been to have had 2 or 3 men to 25 or even 30 women. I think women generally are more likely to want to take up something new when we retire and we're not too worried about showing our ignorance of a new subject or 'losing face.' Maybe that's why we're supposed to live longer than men after retirement

I wonder when I will go through CityLit's doors again. As an elderly, vulnerable, person I've been self-isolated for 10 weeks. Who know how many more?

68 VERA LYNN* PROMISED WE'D MEET AGAIN -- AND WE DID

March 17th 2020 was the last time we were out and about and the last person we saw up close was an AA mechanic. We had gone to the local Waitrose and, when we came back to our car, it wouldn't start. We called the AA and the mechanic told us that, after several good years, the battery had given up and we needed a new one. Fortunately, he carried a replacement in his vehicle.

Since then, the only other people Josh and I have seen in person are the concierges of our flats and the supermarket delivery people– one very jolly woman driver and the rest rather dour men.

Now that there has been some relaxation of lockdown, the Sunday before last we met with our younger son, Bernie, outside Tate Britain and last Thursday we met with our older son, Simon, in the courtyard of our flats – both at the required 2 metres.

We're not a great family for kissing and cuddling but I really missed not being able to give them a hug and getting a hug back.

Louise, who lives in the Basque Country is hoping to come to the UK in the summer, even if she has to stay in a YMCA hostel and meet us in our courtyard, and we hope that Jane, who lives in Switzerland, will be able to pop over too.

Happy Days!!

*Sadly, on June 18th 2020 Dame Vera Lynn died aged 103. Those of us who lived through WW2 owe her an immeasurable debt for keeping up our spirits during those troubled times

The boys had a lot more hair then!! Simon is now almost 60 and Bernard is getting on for 58. Neither of them became an architect or a builder.

69. RACKETEERING AND BAKING POWDER

As soon as it became clear that the coronavirus pandemic was here to stay, staple items vanished from supermarket shelves. Wherever you went, there were long shelves empty of toilet paper, sanitisers and bacterial handwashes. The two back-to-back produce stands in the local Tesco were empty except for one watermelon. I bought in in desperation, but it lasted forever. I don't think I ever want to eat watermelon again.

On eBay, someone was selling a £10 pack of 24 rolls of toilet paper for £49.99 + postage and you could buy a £3 sanitiser for £30.

When the vulnerable were finally allowed to meet one other person outside, we met with our elder son in our courtyard. He had asked for my recipe for Rock Cakes previously but had unfortunately used bicarbonate of soda instead of baking powder. They tasted so awful he had to put them on the compost heap.

I thought I would make him some Fruit Scones using the same recipe I'd been using for years. It calls for soaking the raisins in orange juice for at least 30 minutes beforehand and I used some juice from some rather sour oranges delivered by the supermarket a few days before. I left one of the scones out for my husband Josh to have with his coffee and caught him spitting it out.

'It's vile,' he said. 'Tastes of bicarbonate of soda.'

I tasted one. He was right. It was awful but I thought it was the sour orange juice the raisins had been soaked in. I binned the scones and made another batch. They were just as bad. Then I realised that when I reprinted the recipe, I doubled the amount of baking powder to be added to the self-raising flour.

I wasn't going to risk another batch, so I made some Rock Cakes instead. Josh likes them because they don't contain sugar, just have a little demerara sugar sprinkled on top.

By now, of course, I had run out of self-raising flour and neither of the supermarkets we can get slots for had any. I looked on eBay. A 1 kg bag of self-raising flour costing £1.50 in supermarkets was listed at £11.99 + postage. No way!! Finally, Tesco listed it but every time I put in on my order, when our grocery arrived it was UNAVAILABLE.

I still have some baking powder left but I thought it possible it had 'gone off' and put it on my order. Needless to say, when our order was delivered it was UNAVAILABLE.

I so wish we weren't elderly and vulnerable, and could go shopping for ourselves. I know we should be grateful we can get supermarket delivery slots but like everyone else, I wish it was all over!!

Roll on the Covid-19 vaccine!!

At least this batch of Rock Cakes worked

70. EXTRAVAGANT – YES! BECAUSE I'M WORTH IT

No, I didn't really need a new breadmaker. There was nothing wrong with my old one, but I fancied a newer model. Because of the coronavirus buying frenzy, and so many of us deciding to bake our own bread, Panasonic breadmakers vanished from Amazon and Panasonic UK, only for a few to appear on eBay at profiteering prices.

Our daughter Louise, who lives in the Basque Country, found one on Panasonic es (Spain). She'd had her old one for at least 15 years and it had begun to leak around the spindle. She tried putting in a washer but it didn't help. As in the UK, the local electrical stores and Amazon es were empty of Panasonic breadmakers. However, before any re-appeared in the UK at list price, she found one on Spanish Panasonic.

I wanted the same model but none was available except at a silly price. Finally, my search for a breadmaker resulted in a pop-up note from Amazon offering one at a sensible price from Belgium. I ordered one at once, but when I looked at the site again, to check that my order had gone through, they were once again unavailable. Luckily, my motto is *carpe diem* and I had seized the moment!!

But it was some sort of con!! After 2 weeks, I contacted the seller who said it had been despatched and then that he had asked UPS to send me a tracking number. I heard nothing more and contacted him again only to be told it hadn't been sent and did I want a refund!! Fortunately, I had ordered via Amazon who are excellent about refunds and I have already had the money returned.

I put the code for the breadmaker into Google and was delighted to find that John Lewis had online stock. It arrived yesterday. It bakes beautifully and has the advantage of a window that lets you see the stage your bread is at.

Anadama bread is a traditional New England bread whose yellow colour comes from the addition of molasses and cornmeal. I used polenta, which is cornmeal made exclusively from *otto file* corn.

This bread is said to have got its name from a hungry fisherman saying 'Anna, damn her' after being served by his wife nothing but cornmeal and molasses for supper, day in day out. In desperation, he (or maybe she) threw in some flour and yeast and so made Anadama bread.

71. TATE BRITAIN WILL OPEN ON JULY 27th

It's great that London art galleries are starting to open, though I'm not sure we'll be brave enough to visit them and risk there being large crowds, even if the galleries themselves are set up to regard social distancing.

As well as *Steve McQueen Year 3*, described as one of the most ambitious portraits of children ever undertaken in the UK, Tate Britain will continue to show the Aubrey Beardsley exhibition which opened on March 4th. Then lockdown was imposed and the gallery closed on March 17th. However, on March 30th BBC4 showed an excellent program by Mark Gatiss about Beardsley, still available on iPlayer.

I knew Aubrey Beardsley's work from his illustrations of Andrew Lang's *Fairy Books*. I can visualise the tall bookcases in the children's section of Whitechapel Library where his books lived. I was always small for my age and had to get a librarian to hand me one down. I assume the publisher didn't use any of his more risqué drawings, but while they were a bit frightening, I loved them.

Since Tate Britain closed, we have been going there for our Sunday walks. It is always very peaceful - the occasional jogger, a few couples with a baby in a push chair and the little Chinese grandfather we meet every week. He leads his toddler grandson up the stairs, round the side and down again; gives us a quick smile and walks on.

Our younger son has cycled over to meet us on a couple of Sundays. When I was taking a series of Art History classes in galleries, I bought a folding stool which was much lighter than those provided by the galleries. We took it with us so we could sit on the bench at the side of the stairs and Bernard could sit on the stool the required 2m away.

After July 27th we'll have to change where we take our weekly exercise. Hopefully, the gallery will be very busy. It might be difficult for us to keep a safe social distance outside.

'THANK YOU KEYWORKERS' and 'SEE YOU ALL SOON' banners
have been put up, with the small white 'TATE BRITAIN IS CLOSED' board
by the front door ready to be removed. The black and white banner
advertising the Beardsley exhibition is on the right.

72. DOWN IN THE DUMP IN WANDSWORTH

Who would have thought our treat of the week would be a trip to the Smugglers Way Household Waste and Recycling Centre in Wandsworth? We still haven't ventured into any shops or Art Galleries and this week we gave Tate Britain a miss. We went to Smugglers Way to dump our broken paper shredder, batteries and electrical bits and pieces instead.

We did, however, take our car to be serviced on Thursday. The garage always gives it a good clean so it's looking pristine – until some flying vandal decides to use it as a toilet!!

We both miss shopping. Of course, it's great being able to get groceries delivered, but we like choosing. The fruit is often not what we would have liked – too large or too small - and only now are our deliveries starting to arrive with everything on the list.

Our favourite shops for wandering around are John Lewis and Ikea with Flying Tiger on my list though not on Josh's. Even if nothing takes our fancy it's good to see something different and we always end up with tea and scones in John Lewis or start with a cooked breakfast in Ikea.

Happy days!! Well – maybe soon.

All of us looking like Masked Bandits as we dump our Waste and Recycling.

73. ABOUT THEN AND NOW

Our writers' circle has been meeting fortnightly for 10 years now and I hadn't written anything for the following Tuesday. We have one rule only, that you have to bring something to every meeting.

After I published my memoir *Woman in a White Coat* I started on a sequel dredging up memories I'd left out, but that was boring. Next I tried my hand at sci-fi - parallel universe stuff - and even went to a writing class at our local library for a couple of terms to develop it, but soon ran out of steam.

I had started writing regularly again on my blog and posting on social media, so I brought those pieces to our circle - at first over coffee and homemade muffins and then, since lockdown, on Zoom. By then I had written some 70 illustrated posts, some our children saw and commented on and some they missed, so I decided to publish them on Amazon, as an eBook and as a paperback on Kindle, under the title *Abby's Tales of Then and Now*.

At age 88, it was time to think about leaving a souvenir behind when I'm gone.

Find my book on Amazon and *Look Inside* for a free taster.

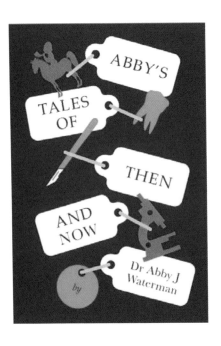

ABBY'S

TALES OF

THEN

AND NOW

by

Dr Abby J Waterman

Dr Abby J Waterman's tales will delight you. Now 88-years old, she writes of her childhood in the pre-World War 2 depression of the 1930s, through to the excitement of the 60s and up to 2020, our lives presently confined by the coronavirus pandemic.

Brought up in poverty in a cold water tenement in the East End of London, she overcomes hardship and discrimination to become a dentist, a doctor, a toyshop entrepreneur, a consultant pathologist and the director of a cancer research laboratory, as well as a wife and mother of four fantastic children.

Following on from her memoir, *Women in a White Coat*, Abby revisits the distant past when her family fled persecution in Eastern Europe. She writes about the present and ponders on what the future may hold.

Her illustrated stories were posted on social media from August 2019 until August 2020. Most of the images are recent and in colour. Others are black and white photographs, dating from the beginning of the 1900s up to the 1960s.

Some of her tales will make you laugh out loud; some will give you pause to think, while others may bring a tear to your eye.

Printed in Poland
by Amazon Fulfillment
Poland Sp. z o.o., Wrocław